Copyright 2021-G.Emslie
All rights reserved, no part of this publication
May be used distributed or transmitted in any
Form or other mechanical methods without the
written permission of the publisher except in the
case of brief Quotations.

Le Congo

A mercenary's tale

Le Congo

By Gordon. Emslie

....

Congo is a fictional account, based on the story of George Stephen a British ex-special forces soldier, who became a mercenary in the Congo, at a time when the Congo was governed by corrupt politicians, warlords, and private armies. This is a story of his adventures and near-death encounters. His diamond smuggling journeys across Europe, and his sadness of lost friends. This is a Congo with the richest potential in diamonds, gold, oil, and other minerals, yet a third-world country, the poorest in Africa due to the ever-presence of corruption at every level of Congolese society and foreign state companies stealing the wealth. You will see this story through the eyes of George Stephen, the main character in this tale of fear and joy, disappointment, and hope.

Chapter 1

The rain bounced off grey pavement slabs, turning them into glistening wet squares. Faceless bodies were hailing fleeing taxis that splashed mini waves onto their shoes as they hurtled past. The lucky few with umbrellas were covering shivering mutts or crying children.

Huddling in a shop doorway I stood with my two pals who, like me had just left the army...Left was the wrong description, I was booted out for striking a superior officer at a booze-up for a retiring sergeant.

Sentenced to one year, reduced on appeal to a dishonourable discharge, and ceremonially marched out of the barrack gates. The only satisfaction I got was the said, superior officer was busted down to acting sergeant.

The army had been my life. I joined as a teenager to escape the grinding poverty and dead-end jobs. Brought up in a city with shipbuilding and fishing as its mainstay.

Strong unions that were out of touch with
what was happening in the world of shipbuilding and would call a strike at the drop of a hat, sending delivery dates back, and sending costs up, failing to modernise had brought its downfall. The ship-buying world had moved on to Asian yards where strikes were unknown and which were cheaper and quicker. Leaving school at fourteen and working on a farm for fourteen hours a day, rain, or shine. A farm in those days was labour intensive with breaks few and far between. The farmer was a Neanderthal. The man stood seven feet five and weighed twenty-two stone, with bushy eyebrows that met in the middle and hair that stood out from the back of his shirt collar.

He had never been to school but had learned to read and write from his mother's 'lodger,' whom she had installed soon after his father was found frozen to death huddled against a tree, where he had sheltered from a blizzard while searching for his dog.

On my sixteenth birthday, I decided that I had enough and joined the army.
I lied about my age, and they didn't bother to check…I had found a home and family.

Over the next few years, I climbed the ladder of promotion and reached the dizzy heights of sergeant in a special forces company, and trained in everything from surveillance, explosives, tactics and everything else that was offered.

With short, sometimes brutal, and bloody 'expeditions' to war-torn ex-British colonies that were forgotten dots on the world map. I'd all the excitement I needed in my life.

But party time was over, now I needed a job… nothing that would get my hands too dirty, and could I accept some spotty-faced youth bawling orders at me, when for the last few years, it's me who did the bawling.

With me was Archie. a short fat Scotsman with a short temper but a heart of gold, and Pete, tall with a mop of blond hair, a guy who knew everything about everything.'

They had both served in my unit and was like brothers sharing the good and bad times had decided to quit the army with me.

'Let's adjourn to the pub. Pete said, 'I think I have the solution to our problem.'
It was 1962 and Harold Wilson was giving a speech from a black and white TV behind the bar. Sitting at the table we shoved pint glasses across a beer-stained wooden top as Pete spread out a newspaper and started reading to us. 'Ex-army personnel required to work overseas on a security assignment….money and accommodation found, tel. for interview. Blah, blah, blah

Archie took a mouthful of beer, wiped his mouth with the back of his hand, and then said.

'Sounds good to me.'

Tossing a coin to see who would check it out.

We all squeezed into the telephone box smelling of urine, covered in graffiti and cards offering sensual massages…What-ever that was? Pete with his semi-posh accent started talking with the guy on the other end. We held our breath till we heard.

'Okay, okay in twenty minutes then, see you then, bye.' Before Pete put the phone down, we babbled out,

'What did he say, what did he say?' like excited children.

Pete leaned back against the grime-covered panes,

'Some guy with a French accent said get your paperwork and pop round to the hotel for an interview.'—It was into a taxi to our rented gaff.

We could smell the room before we unlocked the door. Housekeeping wasn't our forte. Wading through the beer cans and empty pizza boxes we recovered the necessary papers. With our discharge papers and passports in our pockets, we were into a taxi to the hotel to enquire at the desk for Mr Engels. A teenage boy with a pimply face and hair plastered to his head, wearing a waiter's jacket that was falling off his narrow shoulders showed us into a small meeting room on the first floor. I went into a smoke-filled room to see a dozen young guys filling out paperwork, chatting and drinking beer at the same time. Engels pushed through the crowd. A short middle-aged, well-dressed man with gold-rimmed glasses: clipboard in hand and a pen behind his ear, looking all the world like a head waiter. Pushing his glasses up he said,

'And you gentlemen will be?'

Sitting at a table, a peroxide-blond elderly waitress brought some beverages, flashing a fake smile showing tobacco-stained teeth. The Frenchman had told us that the 'beverages' were free. That probably accounted for the 'no hurry attitude' of the guys in the room, taking full advantage of the offer.

The Frenchman explained that the job involved security detail at a diamond mine in the Congo, working shifts to stop the locals from stealing anything that wasn't nailed down.

Archie lowered his glass and stared at the Frenchman,

'How much?' Engels paused and glanced at his clipboard, then stated that an amount of five hundred American dollars per week would be paid into a UK bank account.

Archie moved closer to Pete and lowered his voice...'Did he say five hundred a week?' The average army pay at that time was less than £800 per month. Engels sat in silence checking our papers and passports, making little jots on his clipboard.

Then stood up and remarked he would return shortly for our answer. Pete looked puzzled.

'It can't be that easy, just guarding a mine against petty thieves. Surely the local cops would do that for half the cost, there has got to be more to it.' Archie took a swig from the beer glass and answered with a grin.'

'Who cares, I would do that job for half the money!'

Engels returned twenty minutes later, with the clipboard and pen at the ready.

'So, gentlemen, will you take the job?' three heads nodded in unison,

Glancing at the clipboard he said,

'Then you will be on a flight to Paris tomorrow, and a flight to Brazzaville in the Congo the next day, your flights and hotel will be taken care of.'

We shook hands and he handed Archie a sheaf of papers with times and instructions. Archie turned to Pete and whispered.

'Where is Brazzaville?'

Pete looked puzzled 'Where is the Congo?'

We packed our meagre belongings and headed for our adopted watering hole in town. The place was packed with serious drinkers. Some old girl was dancing to invisible music in the middle of the floor, staring at the brown-stained ceiling with her arms waving in the air, it was that kind of bar. Pete grabbed three beers and found a table. 'What do you think guys?

Sounds too easy for that amount of money eh.' We started to get into our usual for and against when an old scruffy-looking guy lurched up to our table.

'I saw you guys at the hotel today.' Archie growled,

'And so,' The old man carried on,

'You do know there is a war going on over

there a dozen wars are happening now over oil, diamonds, and land.' The old man broke into a cackle. Pete muttered,

'Buzz off.' The old boy wandered back into the crowd still laughing. We looked at each other and Pete stated. 'It did seem like a lot of dough for just watching a mine in the middle of the jungle,' Archie replied,

'What are our alternatives?'

'We could get a job as parking attendants,' Pete answered.

'The council is permanently advertising,' Archie shook his head. 'The council has issued stab vests to the attendants!' Grinning he said,

'It's probably safer in the Congo,' he paused and scratched his unshaven chin,

'Look if we don't like what we see we will hop on the next plane back to Blighty, agreed?' we lifted our drinks and nodded. 'Okay, all agreed!'

The next morning at Glasgow airport joining a queue for the Paris plane. I recognised some of the faces from the hotel. Some of the guys were suffering from hangovers and fell asleep before the plane left the ground.

A short uneventful flight later we touched down at Orly Airport. Bored-looking customs men barely glanced at our passports.

We walked through into the huge concourse and were impressed at the size of the place and style, with glossy fashion shops and cafes with outside tables filled with couples wearing sunglasses, and men with pink sweaters over their shoulders, tied loosely across their chests. They seemed to be watching people watching them—very French. After a couple of overpriced drinks at the plush airport bar, served by a teenage Vietnamese bar girl who said she spoke English and another four languages. Archie looked puzzled.

'How can she remember all the languages,' he shook his head, gulped beer then said, 'It takes all my efforts to speak English.' Taking a taxi to the allotted hotel in the Les Olympiades district on the northern edge of Paris. When I said hotel, I should have said a fleapit with a blinking illuminated hotel sign hanging lopsided on the front of the entrance. A couple of 'Mademoiselles' in short skirts and high heels, standing by the entrance smiled at us as we walked in. The hotel owner, a short obese Moroccan with a mouth full of bad teeth and grey hair to his shoulders approached us in the lobby which had a badly stained carpet with a musty smell. A drunk old man sitting at the lobby table with his head on his chest was snoring and coughing. The Moroccan nodded toward the old man.

'It's the waiter's day off.' Then with a knowing grin said, 'You guys off to the Congo.' Archie nodded. The Moroccan stepped back and let out a rasping laugh, followed by a fit of coughing. Pete snapped,

'Piss off, you are cheering us up,' then we all laughed, even the Moroccan grinned.

After a sleepless night kept awake by a noisy air condition unit and shouting drifting from the lobby.

The next morning after a cup of strong coffee and beans on burnt toast, we set off in a sombre mood. Nobody spoke in the taxi to the airport as we harboured our thoughts. We drove out of the city and into the suburbs and estates then past golf courses and farms. An hour later the landscape changed to rolling fields and the land was so flat that you could see all around for miles. Driving into a small private airfield. Sitting on the tarmac,
away from the usual small micro-lights, gliders, and two-seater planes, stood a twin-engine World War Two Dakota. Painted in green and grey looking like a prop for a war film. I held my breath as I remember watching the programs on air crashes with old twin engine aircraft.

Chapter 2

At the Airport check-in waiting for us was the Frenchman Engels, he pointed to the guys standing behind us, and said,

'Gentlemen, here are your colleagues.'

We looked around at the queue behind us, about a dozen guys were waving and giving a thumbs up. The Frenchman leaned up to me and whispered,

'I have told all these guys that you are in charge, you are the Sergeant Major.' He winked as he walked away. Archie grinned,

'Does this mean we have to salute you?' Then he stuck up two fingers.

Most of the guys were quite young, Kids that went from basic schooling to the army. Most were from deprived areas of the northeast. Towns and Cities that couldn't modernize their once world-beating industries, now found that Asian markets were producing their goods faster and cheaper. There were no jobs for youngsters leaving school. The choice was the dole office or the army.

Given three meals a day, free uniforms, and a bed. All their needs were taken care of. So, after a few years when they left the army and ventured into civilian life, some were like lost sheep. Others made the effort to adjust, applying for jobs, but what insurance office needs a tank commander? An explosive expert or a highly trained sniper?

Three guys were from a special forces unit that had been disbanded after a massacre in some African village done by a drunken band of soldiers from a different tribal group that they had been training.

When an advert came up for ex-military people, many jumped at the thought of organised life—with some well-paid adventure thrown in.

Shaking hands and exchanging names, we boarded the plane. One or two saluted me, they were all ex-army, and like us looking for something to do without getting their hands too dirty. The flight attendants were like models, straight out of a fashion magazine. Dressed in tan fitted suits with red caps and matching shoes, immaculate makeup and a fixed smile that showed high maintenance dazzling teeth. They constantly kept everyone topped up with drinks and rejected marriage—and other less decent proposals.

After a seven-hour flight, with a one-hour break to refuel at a military airport plastered with French language signs and one landing strip of tarmac that disappeared into the dense jungle in the distance.

Looking through the window, I saw several high steel towers reaching into the cloudless sky above the trees, like spiders' legs with enormous circular disks, like TV receivers, only ten times wider, all facing East—Military listening posts.

I watched long columns of tribesmen, wearing French army uniforms, being drilled on a concrete parking area the size of a tennis court, by two tough-looking foreign legionnaires wearing kepis. Every few moments one would march up to an unfortunate recruit, stand nose to nose and yell so loud that I caught some of the words from a hundred yards away.

We weren't allowed to leave the plane for a smoke or to stretch our legs. Everyone complained. Two black soldiers dressed in army uniforms with rifles on their shoulders stood smoking at the foot of the steps from the aircraft. Some guys went into the toilets for a smoke, making the whole aircraft stink of tobacco.

The French air hostesses were replaced by black girls in the same uniforms, but wearing black Muslim headscarves. Later in the day, we landed at Brazzaville airport. And stepped off the plane into a sweltering oven that was the Congo. We were led through customs without anybody being questioned or searched.

Stepping through the glass exit doors into the overpowering heat. The place was swarming with Congolese army soldiers, in different uniforms, and women selling bottles of water from cool boxes. Some soldiers were wearing American army dress jackets. Others in French colonial uniforms.

One young guy wore a Superman tee shirt covered with cartridge belts and carried a heavy-duty machine gun. Most of

them looked like teenagers, wearing various sizes of uniforms, and holding rifles that seemed longer than them.
A Belgian officer strode up to our group and speaking in English with French accent,

'Welcome to the Congo, step over to this hanger...please.'

He pointed to a huge aircraft hangar covered in rusting corrugated sheets. The heat made the air shimmer off the tin roof. Guarded by a solitary black security man sitting in an open-top Jeep, holding a rifle in one hand and a beer can in the other. The officer escorted us over to the hangar. He pointed to a personal door at the side of the enormous plane entrance doors, and said,

'Here is where you will get your uniforms and weapons.' French music was coming from the distance.

In the gloomy and dusty interior laid out on long narrow tables like decorator's pasting tables were piles of assorted French military clothing. The footwear was in tea boxes, with second-hand boots matched by tying the laces together. Other boxes consisted of everything from white tennis shoes to slippers. We were kitted out with shorts, a brown short-sleeved shirt with lighter patches where the last owner's name had been removed, and a red flat cap. At the end of the table was a pile of various World War One bolt action rifles. As the guys shuffled in line to the end of the table with an armful of kit, a rifle was laid on the top.

One guy was handed a rifle of unknown make with a ticket hanging from the trigger guard scribbled in French saying 'Dangereux ne pas utiliser.' (Dangerous. Do not use.) Holding our kit, the Belgian officer lined us up outside on the tarmac. We counted fifteen guys. An ancient yellow American school bus with a cracked windscreen was waiting.

The driver was an old man smoking a cheroot, with a sign above his head in French saying. 'Ne pas fumer.' The officer announced.

'You are to go to the diamond mines at Mbuji Mayi. A chorus of voices responded. 'Where.?'

The common language was French, and luckily some of the guys had a schoolboy understanding. An older British soldier approached me, stuck out his hand, and smiled,

'Hi, I am Ben, before I joined the army,

I lived with my parents in Paris, they were both teachers and only spoke French at home, so for most of my teenage years I only spoke French.'

That was good news to me, I promoted the smiling Ben to adjutant and he was a goldmine when it came to dealing with the Congolese troops who didn't understand English — or didn't want to understand.

Chapter 3

Setting off on a smooth tarmac road with French speed signs on an empty motorway apart from the occasional wild pig bolting out of the jungle and disappearing into the other side, and a couple of women with babies tied onto their backs walking up the slow lane pushing a rickety wooden cart piled with firewood and plastic containers of brown water.
A couple of hours later the bus turned off the tarmac road to journey onto a wide bumpy cinder track that passed for a road with dense jungle on either side shutting out the sun. The bus swerved the many potholes. At every other mile, we saw native women and children carrying bundles of wood and plastic water tubs on their heads, strolling around dead animals at the side of the road. Several hours and many breaks later we neared our destination. It was becoming dark as we passed a huge shanty town of corrugated tin 'huts' with chimneys that were metal pipes poking out of the tin roofs, belching clouds of smoke into the dark sky, almost blocking out the light from the moon. Ten minutes later we arrived at the town of Mbuji Mayi.

Driving through the main street full of music, street markets, and a strong smell of cooking. Groups of drunk Congolese soldiers and local women were staggering up the middle of the street. Two minutes later we arrived at a large concrete area the size of a tennis court on the edge of town surrounded by concrete army barracks. In the stifling humidity, we lined up tired and hungry, when, striding towards us was a huge middle-aged black guy dressed in a black uniform and flat cap, pistol at his side and a major's baton under his arm. Followed by two rifle-carrying guys wearing the same uniforms. A label on his shirt said security police in French. Speaking perfect English, he announced,

'Hi, my name is Bingo, and I am the boss man here.' He had a huge grin with perfect white teeth. His wide thick neck had a tattoo of a snake that curled around his neck and the head joined the tail under his chin.

He gave a half-hearted salute, then led us to a large single-story concrete barracks with a corrugated tin roof. Inside was lit with flickering low-power bulbs that shone on rows of metal hospital beds with small metal cabinets at the side of each one, separated by a hessian curtain. The whole place stank with a mixture of urine and bleach. Standing at the doorway, he opened his arms,

'Welcome to your home.'

Then burst out laughing as he walked away, followed by his grinning escorts.

We were too exhausted to complain. Each guy chose a bed that had a thin futon mattress covered with a single khaki blanket, then put our stuff in the metal side cabinets or shoved it under the bed and drew the hessian 'curtains.' I was so beaten I collapsed on the bed.

Awakening to the sound of whistles and shouting, I realized my arms and legs were covered in tiny bites, I had been too tired to pull over the mosquito netting. Other guys were waking up to sweltering humidity and started to moan about the bites.

The door at the end of the 'shed' opened
and in strolled three local tribeswomen carrying bags, buckets, brushes, and big plastic bags. One wandered up and said in broken English.

'You boss man, me Rose, boss woman,'
then she and the other women burst out
giggling.

Rose was a short plump woman with upper arms the width of a man's leg, and a smooth round face that made her look younger than her forty years. Her huge afro-style hair was full of coloured combs and pencils, sticking out like battleship guns. She had a permanent smile that showed a mouth full of gold teeth, a couple missing and the rest was various shades of brown.

All the men trudged out onto the tarmac outside the barracks. Archie, my second in command did the count and then complaining that we were all starving, he said,

'Where is breakfast?' The woman called Rose pointed down the road toward the shanty town. Just beyond the square was a Congolese army compound.

'In there... good food.' She came closer and
whispered. 'Don't leave money or anything personal or valuable, the cleaning women don't get paid much, and have kids to feed.' Holding a hand over my nose, her breath stank of marijuana mixed with last night's curry. I shouted out.

'Ok, guys if you have money or anything you deem precious, keep that with you.' A couple of guys went back inside.

As we walked in the searing heat to the canteen, the humidity was stifling, it didn't seem to affect the locals. We passed Congolese soldiers wearing army jackets and steel helmets. One guy wore a padded Russian-style hat with flaps and a French football scarf

After breakfast of meaty curry washed down with local beer, I met with two Belgian officers. Franke, the commandant of the Congolese soldiers, and Ernest, the officer in charge of the mine. Ernest gave me the keys to six army jeeps, and then he and all the guys piled into the jeeps and set off for the mine, only four miles through a beaten-earth track in the jungle. Leaving the village, we entered the jungle to the noise of screaming monkeys and birds. A canopy of treetops interlocking high above the dirt 'road.' Like driving through a gloomy Cathedral that shuts out the sun. Twenty bumpy minutes later we suddenly emerged out of the gloom into the bright searing sunlight and the noise of diesel generators. A huge space, the size of a football field was cleared of jungle and had a high wire fence surrounding the perimeter keeping the jungle back with searchlights every hundred metres. The wide double gates were manned by Congolese soldiers. Beyond the fence was an endless green jungle that stretched to the horizon. This was the diamond mine we had to protect. We drove across the cracked concrete towards the mine with brown vegetation reaching from the cracks for the life-giving rays of the sun.

A horse-shoe-shaped cavernous mine entrance led into the black entrance of a large tunnel, big enough for a small truck, dug into the side of the jungle-covered mountain with a narrow single rail bogie track running along one side leading from the tunnel.

Voices were coming from the tunnel.

Ernest threw his cigarette butt onto the dust and crushed it with his boot, and said,

'The shift is coming out, now I'll show you your job.' As he spoke four black miners wearing yellow hard hats, loincloths and boots with no laces pushing an empty rail cart came out of the darkness of the mine blinking in the bright sunshine. Close behind them another twenty native miners carrying small bags appeared covered in grey dust, like ghosts out of the gloom. They trudged to the perimeter and lined up against the wire fence, putting their bags and water bottles on the

ground and putting their hands on their heads or against the wire fence.

'Ok,' the officer addressed us, 'Watch very carefully, this is what you are here for.' Six Congolese soldiers started to search the miners with an officer closely watching the soldiers. The search took ten minutes, they looked in the bags, in their hats and hair, in the shorts and boots. At the sound of a whistle, the soldiers stepped back, and the officer shouted out in French a short speech that sounded like he had said it a thousand times before. The 'speech' lasted less than one minute, and when he finished, I turned to the officer with a puzzled look,

'What was that speech all about,'

he looked at me with a smile.

'That's the speech you will give every shift,

'Basically, ' he said. 'I told the miners that if any man is found to have a stone containing a diamond concealed on his body, he will be marched into the jungle...and shot.'

I wondered, *was he serious?* Ernest stepped back, taking a cigarette packet from his uniform top pocket,

he proceeded to light up and blow smoke into the air and said,

'See, that was easy.' looking puzzled, I said,

'The miners can shove one up their arse, or maybe swallow a small one.' The officer grinned,

'True, but we have an army of informers whom we pay a large bounty to turn them in. Plus, there are very few outlets here that will risk taking the stones, and if we catch them, we will shoot them also.' I looked shocked and said,

'Have you caught any?'

As we started to walk back to the jeeps, he stopped and informed me with a grin.

'There are a lot of widows in Mbuji Mayi. He grinned again and said, If you or your men need washing done...or anything more personal.' he smiled as he got into the jeep,

'Your men are here to replace the Congolese soldiers. It's a question of trust, in the past, some of the soldiers got together and bought diamonds from the miners, then sold them on to the Arab diamond dealers.' He lowered his voice, 'When the scheme was uncovered, three soldiers, an Arab dealer and two miners were shot by order of the Belgian businessmen and a Congolese government minister who owned the mine.' He tapped his nose, it's a question of trust—you start tomorrow.'

The next morning around nine It was already forty-five degrees. We all had breakfast and then dressed in the French army kit and carrying the world-war-one, bolt action rifles,

piled into the jeeps, and drove through the

rutted jungle track to the mine.

A group of tribesmen were at the gates looking for work, but I had been told they belonged to the tribe that dealt with the Arab traders willing to pay for stones that contained diamonds. I noticed that several had only one arm, cut off at the elbow. A soldier told me that they were in constant war with another tribe and if one group caught some of the other group, they would cut off their arm or sometimes a hand, or sometimes—their head! He explained that some tribes had been in constant war with each other over a long-forgotten feud, with outbreaks of fighting that resulted in hundreds of deaths. He grinned and said,

'Like Congolese birth control. The Belgian was waiting to give me a box of keys, plans of the mine and various outbuildings and a thick sheaf of papers. I opened the gates and put two men in charge of the comings and goings. Ernest handed over a box of walkie-talkies and spare batteries with chargers.

The talking was abruptly broken by the noise of machines starting up. Lights on the perimeter fence lit up and a huge generator came alive, like some prehistoric monster awakened from its sleep, pouring out clouds of black diesel smoke into the clear sky.

Meanwhile, I was to meet the local foremen who ran the whole show that afternoon at the beer hall. I spent the day learning the layout of the mine and talking to the British mercenaries, dishing out the walkie-talkies and testing them out to make sure everybody could communicate if a situation arose. As I did my rounds I noticed some tribesmen at the fence, they were not the usual type, they had scars on their chests and foreheads, and there were six of them, carrying spears and long machetes stuck into their loincloths. I was told these were from a tribe that ate monkeys...and their enemies from time to time. Going up to the wire I shouted,

'Hi.' And then gave a thumbs up. They started giggling like children and gave me a thumbs-up. Then as if a signal had been given, turned, and disappeared into the jungle.

I was told that these were the locals who would pick up anything lying around. Other natives would come to the wire fence and ask for cigarettes, then pull out modern lighters, shaped like grenades or pistols.

Chapter 4

At the end of the shift, a whistle sounded. The miners trudged out and lined up against the fence. I shouted, 'OK guys, search them.' Three of our guys put down their rifles and started to pat the miners down looking under the hats and searching their boots. They didn't seem keen on doing the job. It was comical, even the miners were smiling. Blowing my whistle I shouted,

'OK, OK. step back.'

I took a deep breath and started the English speech I had prepared the night before.

'Any miner found to conceal stones containing diamonds will be marched around the perimeter twice, he will be bent over and receive a good kick up the arse with a size ten boot.' All the Brits. burst out laughing. The miners looked puzzled, few understood English, and the ones that did translate the speech to the others slapped each other's

shoulders, laughed and put their hands on their behinds.

A couple of army buses were at the gates to take the miners to the shantytown. I left six men with supplies to guard for the night and the rest set off back in our jeeps.

After a welcome shower and a change, I sauntered into a steaming hot evening at the beer hall. The large ex-barracks were lit with flickering low-power bulbs by a noisy generator at the back of the building. Inside was gloomy, smelling of stale beer and marijuana with lots of noise. Filled with Congolese soldiers and local women

in various stages of drunkenness.

Above the chatter, an out-of-tune piano was being played by an old man who looked like Ray Charles, complete with a shaven head and dark glasses.

His singing in French was drowned out by the chatter of the crowd.

At the bar I got a local beer and met two of the local foremen from the mine, these were the men that the Belgian, Ernest, affirmed would fill me in on the workings of the mine.

They both shook my hand and said,

'I am Pell, he is Rall.'

They looked like twins, same short hair and wearing matching French army shirts and combat trousers.

We left the bar and pushed through the throng to a table. Rall left saying,

'I'll be back in two minutes.'

I Watched as he pushed through the mass of drinkers to a table with some local women who were drinking and playing cards. I took a mouthful of warm beer and turned to the other guy,

'Speak any English?'

He smiled and replied in perfect English;

'I went to the missionary school.' He leaned over the table and whispered. 'Look, before Rall comes back, don't trust him, you come to me with any problems,

I know things that Rall doesn't know.'

Rall appeared. He screwed his nose up as he looked at my glass, 'Why are you drinking the local stuff?' Shaking his head, he leaned over the bar and spoke to the barman, the next minute a glass jug with a clear brown beer appeared. I took a mouthful of the cool beer.' The barman shoved his hand out.

'That will cost you two American dollars a glass jug...upfront.'

I almost choked on the beer. Now I knew why everybody drank the local beer at twenty-five cents a pint. I pulled a face and paid the two bucks. Then we got into a conversation. Telling me the ins and outs of the set-up at the mine, Pell said,

'I need a leak.'

As soon as he left Rall whispered,

'Look, don't trust this guy with anything, come to me with any problems,' he winked,

'I have the contacts. 'We all carried on drinking until I started to see double. I emptied my glass, and slurred,

'Time for home.'

'No No,' said Pel 'Come back to my house in the compound, plenty of French beer...and my sister wants to meet you,' standing with a wobble then shaking my woozy head,

'No thanks, it's back to the barracks for me.
I stumbled out into the cool air of the night,
and staggered ten meters...then the next thing I remember is waking up on a straw bed in a hut. The place was lit by paraffin lamps,
and the smell of paraffin filled the room. A woman was leaning over me, her breath almost knocked me out, she had some gold teeth, one missing tooth and the rest was brown.

'Rose where am I,' she beamed,

'You were robbed, your money is gone. I saw them as I walked down the street to the beer hall, going through my pockets, two guys ran off when I shouted at them, it was too dark to recognize them.' She put a finger to her lips and looked up.

'One of them was wearing a NY cap.' Her face broke into a wide smile. 'I had to pay a couple of kids to carry you back here.' She stuck her hand out, grinned and said, 'You owe me two dollars,' she stuck her hand in my face and frowned

'Would you rather that I left you in the dust?

I forced a smile,

'Rose if the robbers stole my money, how can I give you two bucks?' She pulled her hand back and stuck it on her hip,
paused then chuckled,

'Then you will owe me three dollars, one extra for waiting for my money.' I struggled to my feet and went out into the fresh air, still groggy; it was almost dawn. Back at the barracks, I recounted the story to Pete and Archie, and said,

'You take the guys over in the jeeps and take the night shift back.'

Chapter 5

The population of Mbuji–Mayi in 1960 was around thirty thousand, with a huge shantytown of an unknown number of inhabitants on the outskirts. People worked on the farms that had been cleared of jungle many years ago by early Belgium farmers, but warring tribes and disease sent the survivors back home to Europe. Most of the local population worked in the mines and various dubious occupations when they weren't at war with each other. Rall told me that his brother worked at a farm in the jungle that had been cleared to grow marijuana! Pulling a shocked face I lowered my voice,

'But what about the police?'
'Who do you think owns the bloody place!'
Rall remarked with a laugh.

The Congo had gained independence, but outside of the cities, things went on as normal. Tribes were ruled by chiefs and elders, as they had been done for the past thousand years. Local warfare continued over long-forgotten disputes. Warlords protected the many illegal diamond mines for a cut of the profits. In the past, Belgium-led Congolese army squads attacked private armies that guarded the illegal sites. After gunfights lasting hours, the gunmen and miners would melt into the jungles, only to reappear a few days later and carry on as usual. Some of the open-cast workings were under the protection of Congolese army officers, who would warn the miners of a planned attack. Corruption was rife, wages and army wages were so low that bribes were a part of life. Apart from serious crimes, a bribe to the police would get you off most minor infractions.

I was told you can get anything in the shantytown if you know where to look...And have the money. I decided to find out if this was true as I wandered into a half-empty beer hall, converted from a barracks to speak with Raj. The guy who owned and ran everything, a tall middle-aged Indian with a huge bushy grey beard and an even bigger yellow turban. The kind of guy who knew everybody worth knowing. Shoving a beer across the bar, he stared for a second,

'What can I do for you?' He asked with a smile. Taking a mouthful of beer, I said.

'Raj, I need certain things that I can't get from the local store.'

'He smiled as he leaned towards me, lowering his voice he murmured,

'What do you need.'

'Another passport,' I said, 'French, if possible, but one that will pass muster at the airport.'

He straightened and screwed his face up,

'Is that it? I'll get you a genuine one, all I need is a photo, I'll even tell you where to get that,' he made it sound all so simple! He stood back from the bar,

'Anything else?' I paused.

'Top up my glass with some Castel beer while I think: OK, I need a pistol with a belt

and holster.' He nodded,

'No problem, I have an Indian friend in the

shantytown who can get you that, but bring plenty of money, American dollars, not those Congo francs!' He wiped the bar with a tea towel and said,

'Now you owe me four bucks'

I sputtered ,

'What!' He put his hand out,

'Yes, two for the beer and two for the info.'

He laughed, 'Nothing for nothing in this place.'

He handed me a strip of paper of an address in the shantytown.

I took a bike taxi to the address in the middle of the shanty town. The narrow street had a smell that stuck to my clothes, a cross between a hundred cooking pots and blocked drains.

The closeness of the shacks made the humidity worse. Many dogs of every breed had the run of the place, snarling and barking. The address was a large wooden hut with a tin roof and smoke billowing out everywhere.

I knocked and an elderly Indian with a grey beard down to his waist opened the door a few inches. He looked me up and down,

I was still wearing my uniform, then said,

'What do you want?

Someone shouted from the back of the shop, the old man opened the door another few inches. I leaned in, and said,

'Raj sent me, he said you can help,' the old man opened the door.

'Come in brother,' then paused with the door half open, and asked,

'Have you brought some money?'

Stepping inside my eyes slowly became accustomed to the gloom of half-light and smoke. A couple of young Indian guys in yellow turbans shook my hand, and asked,

'What do you need?'

A young girl dressed in a bright yellow sari and a wrist full of gold bangles came through a hessian curtain with plastic cups of coffee. We all sat cross-legged on a carpet. I explained that I needed a pistol with a belt and holster. The guys looked at each other grinning.

'Is that all?' The older guy uttered,

'I thought you were looking for some heavy-duty stuff.' Grinning, he slapped my leg, 'Come on.' He led me through a curtain to the back of the shop.

The room was lit with oil lamps. It took a minute for my eyes to adjust to the gloom and my nose to the smell. On every wall were hanging AK47s, handguns, bulletproof vests and low and behold, a World War Two British officer's revolver, with a holster and ammo belt.

'How much,' I asked, the Indian stared at me for a second, then answered,

'You want this antique? make me an offer.' Without hesitating I said,

'Twenty dollars.' He tore the gun off the hook. *I should have offered ten!* It was in perfect condition. He handed me a box of shells. I nodded to the rifles on the wall,

'How much for an AK47 with a couple of clips?' he paused for a moment,

'Russian made or Chinese copies?'

'What's the difference.' I asked. He smirked,

'About thirty dollars.'

I suggested...hopefully!

'What about a swap for the French rifles my men were given.' His mouth curled into a smile as he patted my shoulder.

'I don't collect antiques; besides, do they still work.?

Paying the bill, I thanked them and declared—'I'll be back for the AK47' he waved answering

'Remember to bring money...there is nothing for nothing in this town.'

Ambling through the maze of alleys, when I spotted the same bike taxi that brought me here. Climbing onto the torn padded seat I joked,

'Have you been waiting for me?'

The 'driver' nodded and said,

'This is not a good place to be if you don't know where you are.' I remarked,

'How come you speak English?' As we moved off, he turned his head,

'I went to Father Murphy's missionary school, but the nun Margaret caught me stealing and threw me out!'

Bumping along the rough pathways, I asked,

'What's your name?'

Half turning his head he shouted,

'Nkow, but my customers call me Joe.' I leaned back into the padded seat,

'OK Joe, take me to the missionary school.' A bumpy ten minutes later, at the edge of the shantytown stood a high-wired compound with a large single-storied tin and wooden shed, reminding me of a Boy Scouts hut. We came to a halt outside the gate and Joe said,

'You go in from here. If Father Murphy sees me, he might take a swing at me.' I strode to the big wooden door, before I could knock the door was opened by a nun, a tall willowy woman with thick glasses and tape holding them together.

'Can I speak to Father Murphy please?'

The nun looked at me for a moment and replied with a soft smile.

'I haven't heard anyone say please for a while. Come in.' We walked into a giant classroom with broken windows taped up with cardboard and bare walls covered with French graffiti. A mob of kids ranging from four to twenty sat at broken desks. A blackboard hung from a wall, covered in French words next to an English translation.

Teenage Congolese soldiers in uniforms stared at me as the nun led me through a door and into a small room. One wall was covered in dusty bookshelves, a couple of broken desks with plastic coffee cups full of pens, and two cats sleeping on an unmade camp bed. A little stout grey-haired priest with spectacles perched on the end of his nose was sitting at one of the desks. He removed his glasses and offering his hand said,.

'Come in dear boy, have you come to confess your sins?' I caught a strong Irish brough. I smiled,

'I am afraid Father that might take some time.'

'Then you're not of the faith?' he growled. Raising my voice,

'No father, I am an atheist.' he swivelled around in his chair, putting his glasses back on, picked up a sheet of writing, and muttered,

'What do you want from me...I am a busy man.' 'I came to introduce myself and tell you that among my men is one or two of your faith who would like to attend Sunday church.

Turning round in his chair, he smiled,

'Certainly, my boy.' He gave me details, then with a serious look, stated,

'There is a collection expected from the French and British, this school needs funding,' I nodded and said,

'There is nothing for nothing in this town.' He shook his grey head and looked puzzled. I paused.

'Father, perhaps we could meet up tonight in the beer hall or my barracks, 'I would like your advice on a few matters.' He peered past me, waved his palms, and whispered,

'Just close the door.' He lowered his voice, 'I think the beer hall at seven would suit me better, ...although it's a place of the devil.' He got up and walked me through the classroom to the door, followed by Margaret the nun. Looking across to the perimeter gate he spotted Joe waiting for

me, he shook his finger and spluttered,

'It's that little thieving bastard.' The nun gave a little cough and muttered,

'Now, Now, Father Murphy, Now, Now.'

Chapter 6

I went back to the barracks for a shower and change. The humidity was a nightmare. five minutes after a shower the sweat was dripping down my back, yet it didn't seem to affect the locals.

I met the soldiers when the jeeps got back, checked the paperwork, and spoke with Pete and Archie. Pete sounded excited when he told me that they were doing the end-of-shift search when he saw one of the miners dropping this on the ground....he pulled out a tiny stone with a shiny rough white diamond in the middle. Pete said,

'I think one of the miners was smuggling this stone but lost his nerve dropping it on the ground before he was searched, do you think it is worth anything?' I turned the 'stone' over and over in my hand staring at the shiny white diamond in the middle.

'It's got to be worth something,' Pete said, 'Or why would he risk being marched around the perimeter then get kicked up the arse!'

We fell about laughing. Wiping my tears, I remarked,

'I know some people who will tell me all we need to know.' I lowered my voice, 'Keep this to ourselves, I don't want to end up in the jungle with a bullet in me.'

Showing them my pistol and belt and then told them that tomorrow we would all have shooting practice to make sure our old rifles worked. I told them about the AK47s and said, 'You'll have some proper firepower soon.' There was a round of sarcastic cheering.

I told Archie and Pete that I was meeting the Catholic priest at the beer hall at seven,

'I'd like you guys to come along.'

Archie said

'I hope it's for a beer and not a prayer meeting.'

We set off early to the beer hall when we strode into the noisy, smoke-filled bar, the place was full of Congolese soldiers, local women and two Belgian officers. Pete and Archie went to join Ben and some Brits. at a table. The priest Murphy was waiting for me with a glass of Coca-Cola untouched on the bar. We shook hands and I ordered a beer, Murphy put his hand on my arm and in a thick Donegal accent whispered,

'I have a bit of a bad chest cough...maybe a whisky would help.' I nodded to the barman. Murphy leaned over to the barman telling him,

'You'll be making that a double,' and winked. When the glass was placed in front of him, with two fingers he fished out the solitary ice cube onto the bar top. His face beamed as he lifted his glass,

'Cheers my friend.'

Sending the whisky over his throat in one go, his eyes watered as he stared at the empty glass, and said, 'So, what does a heathen want from me?' He paused and put a hand to his chest. 'But first, you had better get me another whisky, bejeezus, I can feel my chest improving as we speak.'

I asked him about the local ceremonies and the local chief and his powers, and he replied,

'The only guy you have to watch is Bingo the chief of the security police,'

he leaned forward and in a hushed voice, 'He runs a protection racket, most of the shantytown enterprises pay him to stay open, don't cross him,' he leaned back winked and touching his nose, said,

'Look, son, all this information is making an old man thirsty.' He called the barman over and handed him his glass. 'Keep them coming.' Pointing in my direction he drawled,

'This guy will pay.' Turned to me with a sly grin and said, 'I forgot my wallet.' He leaned against the bar and let out a loud belly laugh.

It then dawned on me, why a middle-aged Irish priest was ending up in the middle of the Congo jungle teaching the local tribesmen and their kids…he was an alcoholic. His posting was the equivalent of sending a man to the moon on a one-way ticket. The Congo was a dumping ground for wayward priests.

Murphy was drunk when I left him at the bar mumbling about dear old Donegal and went to join the guys at the table.

The Indian barman came over and grumbled. 'Who's going to pay for the Irishman,' I nodded and whispered,

'One more whisky, then throw him out!'

Murphy started to sing Danny Boy above the noise of the crowd, which went on for two minutes but was abruptly ended as he was unceremoniously thrown out.

The next day I went with the guys in the jeeps to the mine, by now everything was working like clockwork. I met with the two local foremen in the canteen, my old drinking partners Rall and Pel. They jumped up and saluted me, a little over the top I felt.

As we sat down with some coffee. I looked at them and remarked,

'You will never guess what happened to me when I left you guys at the bar,' Rall picked up his coffee and started drinking. Pel asked

'Did anyone see who robbed you?'

I was puzzled;

'How did you know I was robbed?'

Rall put his cup down and nodded.

'News travels fast, but we will keep our ears open boss.'

We arranged the Brits. in twos to try out shooting at imaginary targets in the jungle with the old bolt-action World War I rifles. Most worked but two wouldn't fire and two kept jamming, some of the guys threw their rifles on the ground, complaining,

'These are useless antiques.'

I quickly responded,

'Don't worry I'll sort the guns out.'

I stayed till the shift ended and all the noisy machinery shut down. The miners came trudging out to the fence, dropped their boxes and cans and held their arms up against the wire fence.

Somebody shouted...'Search.' My guys started searching the bags and hats, pockets, and boots. Archie jabbed my arm and pointed to a dust-covered miner;

'I think that's the miner who dropped the stone.'

He pointed to a tall young miner with tribal scars on his face and wearing a Congolese soldier's flat cap. I nodded to Archie,

'Search that guy again and let the rest of the miners get on the buses.'

Pete and Archie grabbed the miner and pulled him into the now deserted canteen.

As he sat on a wooden bench, we surrounded him. He was covered in fine dust that flew into the air as he sat down. Archie growled,

'Ok, what have you got hidden, give me what you are hiding, or we hand you over to the Congolese officers, they will take you into the jungle beat the shit out of you, then shoot you, innocent or not, to them it's entertainment.' He dropped his head.

'Please, boss.'

He spoke in fractured English, and his hands were shaking.

'I have two wives and seven kids to feed.'

He started sobbing, putting his head on the table, and said, 'Please boss let me go home to my family.' I bent over to speak into his ear,

'Last chance! What have you taken from the mine, or I hand you over to the Congolese.' He slowly stood, stepped back from the table took his flat cap off, turned it outside and pulled out two small shiny stones, putting them on the table, then reached down the back of his shorts and tugged out a cloth bag. Another tiny stone spilt onto the table. Archie looked puzzled.

'Gee, is he going to pull a rabbit out of his arse next?' We all laughed except for the miner. Pete was still laughing when he looked at the miner and said,

'Let's get serious you know what this means old chap!' The miner looked down at the floor, and Archie said,

'Well, it means that at the appointed hour, you'll be marched around the perimeter twice, bent over and kicked up the arse with a size nine boot.'

Archie Pete, and I fell about with laughter. laughing so much, tears ran down my face.

The young miner stood looking puzzled. I dried my tears and we all sat down.'

'Ok, buster.' I began to speak as he stood up and said,

'No, not buster, me Nkomo, you boss man.' Pete smirked,

'He boss man...yeah right.' I growled,

'Look Nkomo all I need is some information, give me the information that I ask you and you will go home to your two wives and seven

kids....or was it seven wives and two kids?

He had wives...Plural and mouths to feed.

'Who do you give the stones to?'

His eyes widened,

'If I tell you who I'll be dead by tomorrow.' I tried to look serious,

'Nkomo my friend if you don't tell me, you will be dead by tonight! then who will look after your brood? Of seven....whatever!

He stared at the floor for a moment, then in a hushed voice said,

'It is an Arab trader from the shantytown, I meet him on Saturday morning at nine, two hundred yards into the jungle road from the end of the tarmac. He gives me ten American dollars or sometimes fifteen if I have more than one stone'

Pete commented:

'Gee, you risked being shot for ten bucks?'

Archie leaned forward and still giggling, said,

'Or a kick up the arse from the Brits.'

We all laughed, and even Nkomo started to

smile. Opening his palms, he slowly shook his head, 'But who will take any stones I manage to get out, I need the money!'

He was beginning to get cocky. I looked at him and smiled,

'I will, but keep your mouth shut or we will all end up in the jungle. I put a finger to my head...Bang bang. When you have a stone with you, put a cigarette behind your ear, and Archie or Pete will search you if I am not there. I asked,

where do you live?' He mumbled,

'In the shantytown.'

The bus had already gone so I said,

'Ok get in the jeep with us.'

We drove back to the compound but dropped Nkomo off at the end where the jungle ends and concrete and tarmac begins. He pointed out where he would meet the trader. I parked the jeep and went into the compound. I was feeling nervous as I checked on the two guards at the gate.

Sitting on my bed thinking about my next move. The whole sleeping area only had a hessian curtain separating the beds, anyone could pull the curtain aside and walk in, you can't exactly 'Knock' on a curtain.

Carefully slipping the stones and the bag out of my pocket, I put them into my, 'under-the-bed safe.'

Guys were coming and going to the showers. A concrete block of six cubicles, each one with a shower head fixed to a wooden pole dispensing warm or cold brackish water.

Two yards further were the latrines. A concrete block with one door for in and another door at the end for out. A plastic pipe ran from the back and led out the effluent three hundred yards through the trees and bush to empty into a slow-moving stream.

The smell was appalling, and over ran with rats. A change of breeze direction would carry the smell to the barracks to join the ever-present smell of cooking. *The curtain could be pulled aside any minute by someone needing to ask me something —How could I explain the stones?* We were supposed to stop smuggling! I had to keep the stones on me or find a safe place to hide them. It was Friday. Tomorrow, Saturday was the celebration day for weddings. Murphy and his nuns blessed the babies, and the recoveries from the local killer diseases and anybody else who gave a few francs to the kitty. I didn't go to the beer hall that night. Sitting on my bed in the dark, thinking over and over in my mind what was I going to do with the trader tomorrow. How was I going to persuade the Arab that I was getting the stones from now on, how would he take it? If the roles were reversed, would I give up a good thing? One anonymous word from him to the Congolese and I am a dead man, along with Nkomo, and maybe some Brits. if they tried to object or stop a kangaroo trial.

Chapter 7

Hardly sleeping that night, I woke at dawn and stepped outside. The morning air was unusually fresh and cool. I had decided that I would tell him sorry and that I made a big mistake, give him the stones and hope that would be the end of it. Pete and Archie came over,' Archie said,

'Do you want us to come with you in case he tries something?' I shook my head,

'No, no. I don't want you guys to get involved in something that can get you shot. Meet me in the beer hall in a couple of hours.' Pete patted me on the head,

'See you in a couple of hours, be careful.'

I smiled and patted my revolver. That was just bravado, I was shaking inside. Getting into one of the jeeps, I turned the key.

Driving into the jungle track, I parked in the bushes and rambled along the wide dirt track that passed for a road, into the shade of the jungle, when, fifty yards along the track I saw a little bearded Arab leaning against a tree, smoking a cheroot. He was dressed in a black dishdasha, a 'dress' that came from his neck to his ankles, like a long nightdress, and a kufi cap. He was holding a bracelet of black prayer beads in one hand. I waved, and said,

'Hi.' He nodded then growled.

'Get lost,' and spat on the ground. I nervously asked,

'Are you waiting for Nkomo?'

Tossing the cheroot onto the ground he straightened up.

'What do you know about Nkomo?'

Taking a deep breath, I said,

'I have come to deliver the stones.' He glared at me for a second as if he hadn't understood what I had just said, and then pulled a gun from his pocket. Pointing it at my head he uttered,

'You know too much, hand over the stones and go, if I see your face again, you're a dead man.'

I took the stones out of my shorts pocket and handed them over saying in a shaky voice,

'Ok man, all is well now, yeah? I'll be on my way.' He snatched the stones and stuffed them into his pocket then glared at me and said something that changed the whole game. He declared with a smirk,

'I have other contacts at the mine.' I looked surprised. The Arab growled and spat out, 'Nkomo is a dead man'—In one swift move, I snatched the gun out of his hand and pulled out my pistol, a move that I had practised many times.

His eyes widened and his mouth fell open as he stepped back in surprise. I can still recall the look of horror on his face as I shot him twice in the chest. As he fell backwards into the bushes, a dark patch formed on his garment, I stood still for a long moment listening to the screaming monkeys in the canopy of trees. Watched by monkeys, witnesses who couldn't testify.

Going through his pockets I retrieved the stones and searched for ID. Who was this guy? Who was going to miss him? Who was going to come looking for him? I was trembling with fear and excitement. Looking all around. In the distance, I watched as threads of smoke from a hundred chimneys curled slowly into the cloudless sky from the distant shanty town.

Picking up his body, and throwing him over my shoulder. I trudged into the dense jungle. Branches tore at my clothes and legs. After a few minutes, I came across a hollow area surrounded by jungle and filled with stinking green water. Heaving his body into the water it quickly disappeared sending up bubbles into the green slime, his gun followed. I stared for a few seconds till the slime settled. A crocodile slid into the water from the far bank. Then I strode back to my jeep, brushing leaves and thorns from my tunic. I had never killed anyone in cold blood before and was still in a state of minor shock as I entered the beer hall.

At a table were Pete, Ben, and Archie with two other guys. Archie stood and muttered,

'You're covered in scratches and there's blood on your shoulder.' He came closer and whispered, 'Did you beat the guy up?' I replied without making eye contact,

'Archie, that guy won't be threatening anyone ever again.' He gave me a blank look, sat, turned to his beer, and didn't speak again. I stood and said,

'I need a shower and a change of clothes; I'll see you guys later.' Walking out into the searing heat I took a deep breath. A putrid smell from the stream was hanging in the air.

I stood under the cold shower for several minutes, trying to get my head in order with what had just happened. It seemed as if I was in a dream, but I knew that what had happened was all too real! I closed my eyes and my mind drifted back to my army days.

Chapter 8

The shooting and sometimes the killing of the enemy didn't trouble me, part of the training was psychological, if killing the 'enemy' disturbed you, or kept you awake with the guilt of taking a human life, then you were a danger to the mission, yourself and more importantly the guys around you. If you faced an armed 'enemy' and hesitated, he would not, that was drummed into you. When I say 'enemy' I am not talking about a trained, motivated soldier, it was more likely to be a poorly armed local, promised a reward to kill a European soldier, and told that he was impervious to their bullets.

Such an instance still haunts me.

On one of my missions in late 1963, my team was flown to Sana'a in Aden and then helicoptered to a featureless, sand-covered hillside overlooking a valley that raised to another hill. The rebels had to come this way to reach the towns on the coast. The British government was secretly assisting the fledgling Aden government to hold back Soviet-backed rebels from taking over the country.

We erected a couple of tents to protect our supplies and ammunition and set up a small World War 2 Howitzer and apart from grenades and rifles, an MG42 machine gun. The scorching sun beat down on the group with only a canvas roof over the Howitzer. Four troopers taking shifts, two on duty and two resting. Archie was the radio man. Pete and Oliver, a Māori New Zealander, took turns scanning the hill on the other side of the valley. To break the boredom, we took pot-shots at vultures circling high in the featureless sky. Everything changed on the sixth day. Shadows retreated yard by yard as the sun climbed into the sky, chasing shadows across the sand, when on the unseen side of the far hill a bugle sounded, it sounded like an explosion in the shimmering air. Waves of screaming tribesmen came charging over the far hill, waving rifles, swords, and banners, they were followed by more and more, until there were several hundred, yelling as they ran down the hill to the valley. The ping of bullets hitting the sand, made us leap to our guns.

Oliver, the New Zealander loaded the Howitzer and fired. The blast landed in the middle of the mob, throwing bodies arms and legs into the air. Archie was calling for help on the radio and Pete was firing into the mob with the machine gun. Yelling changed to screams and moans as the Howitzer shells were exploding. The steady chatter of the machine gun caused chaos and the charge slowed, the tribesmen at the rear paused, turned, and fled back up the hill, dropping the banners and weapons as they ran in terror.

The first few rows kept coming, some had reached the valley and were running up the hill towards us, and a few had stopped to fire their ancient flintlocks and modern AK49s. The Howitzer had stopped firing. The machine gun mowed down the nearest few, the grenades stopped the rest. The shooting had stopped, and the few rebels that were halfway up the hill were easily cut down. Pete had a bullet hole in his boot. Oliver was lying by the Howitzer—Dead! A stray bullet had pierced his neck, cutting a main artery. The irony was, he was the only one wearing a bullet-proof vest. Shielding my eyes, I watched vultures circling in the cloudless sky. On the far hill lay the dead and dying.

The sun was dipping below the horizon as the screaming and groans from the dying were becoming less, apart from one guy whose moaning seemed louder. I decided to put him out of his misery, striding down to the valley, then up through the bodies and bits of bodies scattered around, I found him, he reminded me of a hippy student, with long hair and a wispy beard, his chest was hit by shrapnel and one leg was cut almost in half. As I stood over him, he closed his eyes and put his hands together as if praying, a silver cross hung around his blood-covered neck. This guy was one of the foreign volunteers helping the rebels. I put the muzzle of my rifle on his forehead—and hesitated. His lips slowly curled into a smile as I pulled the trigger.

The image haunted me for years. That night I was awakened by the sound of wailing coming from women and old men searching through the bodies. Peering through the blackness, dots of flickering lights were moving through the bodies like tiny lights from a crowd at a rock concert. As dawn rose, the smell of death drifted across the valley, wild dogs were eating human flesh and hordes of Vultures were hopping from body to body. Archie threw a grenade; the blast made the birds fly into the air like a huge dark cloud, and the dogs fled in terror.

At midday, the helicopter arrived, creating a sandstorm. We lifted Oliver's body into the craft, then spiked the Howitzer with a grenade down the barrel. Lifting off in a cloud of whirling sand, we flew over the valley, I looked down at the carnage below— The dogs and vultures had returned.

Chapter 9

Sitting in the radio shack in the compound, the crackling voice was saying that a massacre was discovered in a village over a hundred miles south of Mbuji-Mayi. The news didn't shock me, the battle between warlords, private armies and mercenaries fighting over oil fields, and gold and diamond mines had been going on for decades since the Belgians gave the Congo independence. Congolese politicians had scrambled for control over the natural resources of the country, the losers were the Congolese people. As I sat listening to the news of Congolese army reports of dead natives found in the jungle as they tried to escape the killers, and mutilated bodies left to rot in the sun, I felt a sense of despair. Yes, my British mercenaries and I had killed but only in self-defence or on rescue missions. Some of the private armies of ex-Congolese soldiers, 'boy soldiers' and rag-tag thieves and drug addicts would kill everyone in a raid on a village. The only ones spared were natives from the same ethnic tribe. The Congolese army comprised mostly Bantu tribes and tended to leave others to fend for themselves. Although Congolese cities are modern by today's standards, beyond the tarmac highways and high-rise buildings, the village tribes lived the same way for a thousand years with ethnic groups in constant war with each other over long-forgotten feuds. My group of British ex-soldiers were being used more and more to quell the risings of Congolese soldiers who were paid to protect villages who rebelled when they hadn't been paid for weeks and months due to government corruption. Some soldiers would rob the villages they were supposed to protect, then disappear back to their villages. A few days after I had heard of the latest raids I was summoned to the compound of Franke, the Belgian officer in charge. The Congolese soldier saluted me as I entered Franke's office. Sitting with Franke was a middle-aged Congolese man dressed in a linen suit, white shirt, and college tie. We all shook hands and he said, 'So, you're in charge of the

English mercenaries, I am Leon Mabate leader of the UDPS.' He paused as if I knew who that was, then said,

'The opposition in parliament.'

Nodding as if I knew, I glanced at Franke and said,

'What has all this to do with me, with respect I am not interested in Congolese politics, I am only interested in guarding this diamond mine.'

Leon shuffled his chair around to face me, then said,

'Last month my father and my uncle were killed protecting their village from a warlord who demanded they pay him for protection, when my father refused, they raided the village and killed him and some of the villagers. Now the survivors pay protection money to live in peace.'

Squeezing his hands into fists, and clearing his throat, he raised his voice, 'I want revenge for my father, find the guy who ordered the raid and kill him!' He paused and pulled a large bag onto the desk. 'Here are half a million American dollars,' Find this guy and if you kill him there is another half million,

I have cleared this with Franke, he is going to put it down as a rescue mission.

We both looked at Franke who nodded.

Leon shoved the bag towards me and said,

'Everything you need to know is in the bag.'

'Whoa, I'll have to speak to my men first,' I said, 'But for a share of a million dollars and a break from boredom, I think they'll go for it.'

Leaving Congolese soldiers in charge at the mine, I assembled the twelve Brits. in the beer hall and put it to them with the offer of a forty-thousand bonus, and another forty thousand if we were successful.

Eleven hands went up, the guy who didn't vote had a pregnant Congolese girlfriend and when he wasn't on duty at the mine, he helped his girlfriend's father run a market stall.

Two days later, Eleven British mercenaries and four Congolese soldiers boarded two battered yellow American school buses, armed with AK-49 rifles, ammunition, a mortar, and the essential crates of beer cans!

Three hours of travelling over roads of beaten earth full of water-filled potholes,
with mud a foot deep in places and surrounded by endless jungle it was getting dark when we stopped two hundred yards from the village. Two Brits. and a Congo soldier walked to the village to find out the situation. Twenty minutes later they strolled out of the gloom, saying everything was quiet.

They had spoken to an elder who told them that four rebels were sleeping in a hut at the end of the village. The other fifty or so were with the leader ten miles away in the next village. The men were tired after the journey, and as it was dark and peaceful, we slept on the bus with two guys on watch. Dawn broke to a chorus of screaming monkeys and clouds of birds rising from the trees, smoke was rising from the chimneys of the huts as we drove into the village and were surrounded by kids and barking dogs.

Marching to the end of the village, we surrounded the hut that held the sleeping rebels. After ten minutes of waiting for something to happen, someone threw a stone at the door, and a minute later a teenage boy stepped out rubbing his eyes, then froze at the sight of a dozen guns pointed at him. He turned to go into the hut when a dozen bullets hit him, a moment later three teenagers ran out with guns. Before they could fire, they were shot in a hail of bullets and joined their colleague lying in the dust. One of the teenagers was still alive and moaning. Before I could stop him, a Congolese soldier stood over him and shot him twice. Several men from the village carried the bodies away, leaving their blood to stain the earth.

The elders we had met showed us huts to stay in and hold our equipment. The bus was driven out of the village and hidden in the jungle a mile away. After checking our weapons and taking up positions around the village we settled down to wait for the enemy to appear. After breakfast made by the women, I sent two

Brits. to head towards the next village and find out the strength of the rebels and their weapons. I learnt a long time ago that the kids of a village were the best spies, the jungle was their playground, and they knew the whereabouts of any strangers.

For a few Congolese dollars a dozen kids followed by a pack of dogs went into the jungle to spy for me. Later that afternoon the Brits. returned to tell me that over fifty 'boy soldiers' and a Congolese guy dressed in a major's uniform were at the village and seemed well-armed with new FN Belgian rifles. An hour later the kids and dogs emerged from the jungle and all speaking over one another told me that four of the rebels were on their way to relieve the four that we had killed.

Taking up positions behind the huts and one of the Brits. was a sniper hidden inside the jungle edge. We heard the rebels before we saw them. Arguing and shouting, their voices travelled in the still air of the jungle.

Walking in single file they emerged from the jungle carrying their rifles over their shoulders. The centre of the village was deserted with the villagers hiding in their huts. Looking around the deserted village the 'boy soldiers' looked at one another, then shouted names, pulled their rifles from their shoulders, and pointed them at the huts.

The snipers bullet killed the kid in front who collapsed as the other three panicked, opening fire in all directions. A hail of bullets from the Brits. in hiding killed the other three. It was all over in seconds. The villagers slowly came out of their huts and stared at the bodies on the ground. Kids ran to the bodies and searched them for money or anything they could trade with each other, and then half a dozen villagers crept to the bodies and stared at them as if expecting them to jump up and shoot them, then carried the bodies away.

I knew that others would come looking for the original four when they didn't return, so I had to prepare for a firefight, but I had the advantage of surprise. Gathering the kids together and handing each one a Congolese dollar, they went into the jungle and would tell me if the Rebels were coming. Nothing happened that day, except the kids returned to tell me that there was fighting between the rebels over a drunken argument after drinking all day. Setting up the mortar to zero into the jungle path that the rebels would have to take to reach the village, then most of the Brits. took to the huts, making holes in the walls at the bottom where they would lie on the floor and could shoot without being seen. One of the Congolese soldiers volunteered to hide off the path and watch for the rebels approaching. I gave him one of the walkie-talkies, I had the other.

Sharing the ammo. and the last of the beer! We settled down to wait. A crackling voice of the Congolese soldier came from my walkie-talkie,

'They are coming, they are coming!'

Shouting for him to return, then shouting at the top of my voice I told the men to *stand by*.

The village was deserted, even the dogs had gone, the villagers had sensed what was coming and stayed in their huts or hidden in the jungle.

Sounds of shouting and cursing from the 'boy soldiers' told me that they hadn't been trained in field tactics.

I signalled to the mortar guy and seconds later a loud explosion in the jungle followed by tree branches flying into the air.

Screams of the wounded were followed by shooting from the unseen rebels. Another round exploded sending screaming hordes of monkeys fleeing from the area and flocks of birds lifting into the air like black clouds. The first of the 'boy' soldiers appeared from the jungle and shot wildly at the village huts, some of them had painted faces and wearing bandanas like mini rambos. A wall of lead from the Brits. sent most of them to join their ancestors. The rest retreated in panic along the jungle path.

Another mortar shell sent them running back in confusion. Leading the Brits we entered the jungle path, over twenty bodies and parts of bodies lay scattered on either side, and a few rebels were badly wounded and moaning for help. I am ashamed to admit I knew what was going to happen next. Two of the Brits and a Congolese soldier walked among the wounded and shot them. I tried to convince myself that this was the only answer. We couldn't take prisoners, and I thought of these guys who had massacred their people and would have killed us if they could. I shouted at my men about the rules of war and the Geneva Convention, no one stopped to listen, the men who knew me, knew I was trying to ease my own concerns, but they knew we had no choice. The Congolese leader dressed as a major was lying in the trees—dead. Shrapnel had severed his leg and he had bled to death. One of the Brits. had a camera and took the 'majors' photo.

The exhilaration of the action had subsided as we returned to the village. The villagers, kids and dogs had magically returned, and the kids ran into the jungle to search the bodies for money or anything they could sell. Tribal instincts returned as some villagers sought revenge by mutilating the bodies.

My first thought was to stop them, but I realised the suffering they had endured and wondered what I would do in their place.

The next few days were resting, drinking locally made beer and eating the food served by a grateful village.

Retrieving the busses, we loaded everything and waved the villagers' kids and dogs goodbye. I handed the elders the last of my Congolese dollars and left, followed by barking dogs. The long bumpy road didn't stop guys from sleeping on the way back to the diamond mines of Mbuji-Mayi and 'home.'

As is usual after a mission, we headed for the beer hall, the converted barracks run by Raj. I got drunk hoping it would wash away some of the memories of the killings. In the morning I stood under a freezing shower with a throbbing head. I had started to suffer from lack of sleep. The faces of men I had killed would visit me in my dreams. When prisoners had to be 'liquidated.' Like a coward I let others do the killing. Many of my colleagues suffered from this, some couldn't take the nightmares and turned to alcohol or drugs. Many ex-special forces who left the army committed suicide, or finished up in mental hospitals. I tried to tell myself that it was a 'job' and if I didn't kill them, they would kill me. I would tell myself as long, as I didn't kill women and children the rest was fair game. I hoped the man in the mirror believed me.

On one mission where we had ambushed the 'enemy.' There had been shootouts, some of the 'enemy' escaped, others surrendered with the wounded. We guarded them until our helicopters arrived to get us out. As my squad boarded, I handed over the prisoners and the wounded to the local militia, and explained to their commander the rules of war. As the helicopter lifted over the trees, I heard sounds of machine gun fire.

Back at barracks. I sat with my commanding officer as he studied my three-page report. Looking slightly annoyed, he said,

'Look old chap, this won't do.' Handing back my report, scratched his head and said,

'I can't give this to the Minister, take it away and bring me back a fairy story, something the Minister will like. You know the drill. No British casualties, enemy melted away taking dead and wounded. Local militia assisted. Locals cheered you off with a thank you. As long, as there were no British casualties, I don't care what fairy tale you give me.' Glancing at his watch as he stood.

'Now, I have a round of golf in half an hour.'

Chapter 10

Handing my report to Franke, he waved me to sit as he glanced through the two pages of my heavily doctored report then nodded to himself and shouted to an unseen soldier to fetch coffee.

'Leon Mabate will be here tomorrow to thank you himself, have you got evidence of the leader's death?'

Putting his coffee down, he rasped,

'And get you men back to the mine, the Congo soldiers you put there are fighting with the miners who went on strike, I had to give them a bonus and move the soldiers outside the perimeter gates before they would return.' Finishing my coffee, I returned to my barracks and a welcome bed.

Late the next day a black Mercedes followed by an open truck of soldiers pulled up in a cloud of dust.

Leon Mabate was dressed in a military uniform as I entered behind him into Franke's office. As we shook hands, I noticed a large canvas bag under the desk. Handing him the camera with the screen showing the dead 'major' a tear trickled down his cheek. Putting the camera down and wiping the tear, he said,

'Now my father can rest in peace, he's been avenged.' There was a moment's silence, and then he pulled up the canvas bag, and said,

'I am a man of my word, here is the money as promised.'
I gave an involuntary shudder as he said,

'I may need to use your services again.'

After he had gone, I patted the bag and said to Franke,

'Now at last, there's an honest Congo official.'

Franke lit a cigarette and smiling said,

Leon Mabate has a 'wage' of Fifty thousand dollars, but lives in a million-dollar villa.'

At the mine, the money was shared with the Brits. I gave the four Congolese soldiers that were with us five thousand dollars each, which was equivalent to six years of army pay. As I expected three Brits. decided to return to the UK. They were the guys who told me they took on the job to pay the mortgage or settle the bills.

Chapter 11

Saturday was a day for celebrations, weddings and divorces, Congo style and generally with a reason to dress up. The women wore colourful wrap-around dresses, while the guys wore long pants with matching tunics and hats to match. The square in front of the compounds was mobbed. Tribesmen came from far and wide. The weddings were the opportunity for relatives to meet and wives to show off their dresses and hairstyles.

The men usually got drunk on the locally made beer and argued with other drunks! Or their wives.

Weaving their way through the crowds came Murphy and the nuns, behind them came a couple to be wedded; the groom was the Congolese soldier who got thrown out of the beer hall for fighting. He was in an army dress uniform; he also had a black eye and a cut over his brow. His to-be wife was a large young woman with huge afro hair holding a tiny baby. Murphy started by sprinkling water over them and shouting in his thick Irish accent,

'If any man objects to these two souls joining in holy matrimony say now, or forever keep your peace.' Margret the nun stood by his side and translated the speech into French for the onlookers. About twenty voices shouted back that he had a girlfriend. The crowd broke into laughter.

Murphy ignored them and droned on about the sanctity of marriage, then the baby started crying. With one fell swoop, the bride reached into her dress and pulled out an enormous boob and stuck the infant to it.

Murphy shook his head, and said,

'I now pronounce you man and wife.'

As the crowd drifted away, the groom stood looking around for someone to tell him what to do next.

The bride, with the baby still stuck to her massive boob turned away into the crowd as the mob started dancing—or more like a shuffle. The drums were going by this time, and everybody was joining in, even Murphy was shuffling around the circle.

The nuns stood together outside the circle with glum faces watching Murphy waving his hands in the air as he joined the throng of bodies.

The circle was getting bigger and bigger with around five or six hundred bodies. Congolese soldiers made up most of the shuffling dancers, half bent over and waving their arms in timing to the drums. Every few minutes someone would shoot their rifle into the air, sending the monkeys screaming high in the trees.

The atmosphere was amazing. Rose was with Queenie, one of her daughters. Wading through the crowd I joined them, shuffling around and waving my arms like a lunatic.

Then as in a sci-fi dream, above the crowd's noise and drums, I heard the whine of bag-pipes...Playing Amazing Grace.

The atmosphere was electric. The dancing went on for an hour or more until everybody was exhausted. Small boys were coming from the shanty town pulling carts with beer and bottles of water to sell to the crowd. Couples holding hands were creeping into the bush.

Then a hush fell over the crowd as half a dozen black-shirted security police dragged a local man into the middle of the square, led by Bingo. Tying him to a pole. Bingo shouted above the noise, reading from a sheet,

'This man stole a goat from his ex-wife and beat her when she caught him.' One of the security men ripped the guy's shirt off, then Bingo produced a long cattle whip.

He stepped back and swung the whip onto the prisoner's back...one! The crowd cheered, and the prisoner flinched as Bingo whipped him three more times. The mob cheered again as he was cut down, collapsing onto the dust, his back drenched in blood.

Bingo grinned at me with perfect white teeth and shouted above the crowd.

'I am the law!' This was justice—Congo style!

Pete, Archie, Rose and her daughter Queenie and I, walked to the beer hall as dusk fell. It felt good to have some fun after the drama of yesterday. Hoping the beer and the company would erase the memory of the Arab falling into the bushes with bullet holes
in his chest.

I rose early Sunday morning and drove my jeep into the Shantytown. The sky was grey with the smoke from hundreds of chimneys. I parked up and walked through the narrow cinder path with a warren of tin shacks that leaned and sagged on each side.

Knocking on the Indian's door, the old man slowly opened the door recognised me, and waved me into the room, two guys were drinking coffee and eating breakfast, and the smell of cooking filled my nostrils. The Indian waved me to sit with them and the old man served me coffee and toast.

'What is it this time boss man,' he spoke without looking up, I put my cup down,

'I need the AK47s.' Finishing his coffee he glancing up, asked,

'You have money?' Smiling I said,

'Nothing for nothing in this town.' He laughed and slapped my shoulder, lifted a corner of the patterned tablecloth, and wiped his mouth, stood, and led me through the hessian curtain to the back rooms. He lit some oil lamps that showed the rifles and guns hanging from the wall. Handing me an AK47 with a wooden butt,

'How does that feel,' he asked, weighing it with my hands it felt lighter than I thought. He nodded, taking the rifle from me.

'Now try this one,' he put the second one in my hands. It was heavier and had a rougher finish. He told me that the first one was Russian-made, and the second was a Chinese copy. I paused for a moment then said,

'I'll take ten Russian models with twenty clips.

'If these are up to scratch,' I said, I'll be back for more.' His face broke into a broad grin.

His helper was tying up the guns and wrapping them in some Hessian. As he was counting the money I had a stroll around the dimly lit room, and then, lo and behold I saw a box with British army markings, it contained explosives with timers, a sort of grenade with a small plastic timer attached, I had used the same ones in training years before. Pointing to the box I remarked.

'How much.'

The Indian grinned and answered

'I have been trying to sell these for years! How many do you want?'—I thought for a moment, *where was I going to need them?* 'I'll take Five,' he looked disappointed when I offered five dollars. He paused then nodded.

Gingerly put them into a canvas bag We shook hands all around. As I went out the door, the Indian shouted,

'Thanks for your business,'

I shook my head,

'You mean my money,' we both smiled. He stepped towards me with a box in his hand,

'Here is a little thank you,'

Handing me a bottle of black-label Johnnie Walker. Raj the beer hall owner was right, you can get anything your heart desires if you know where to go. I was helped to put the weapons and everything in the jeep and covered them up, then drove back to the barracks.' Shoving everything under my bed, then went down to a half-empty beer hall. I got a beer and spoke to Raj.

'Where is everybody?' He lifted my beer glass and wiped the bar top with a wet cloth.

'There are all with Father Murphy, they go for his hell-fire sermons.' He picked up my beer and topped it up, then put it in front of me saying,

'Most of them attended his school to get a basic education and learn English, they used to be funded by the church but the Cardinal based in Kinshasa was told that Murphy was drinking most of the cash, So, he cut the money off last year, and now Murphy must charge a small fee from the kids' parents and there are many orphans.'

The light was fading as I walked back to the barracks. The next few weeks were uneventful, with Nkomo passing me more stones.

Then one evening the Belgium officer summoned me to his compound. He lit up a cigar, blowing smoke up to the brown-stained ceiling, he paused as if he was thinking about what to say. Leaning over the desk he lowered his voice and said,

'Understand, this has nothing to do with me, it comes from headquarters.' He put his cigar into the cracked marble ashtray, slowly put his glasses on then read from a sheet of official-looking documents. He spoke as if he was addressing a crowd.

'All British soldiers were to swap places with the Congolese army soldiers for one week. The Congolese were to conduct a thorough search of the buildings, inside the mine and question the miners.' When he had stopped speaking, I asked,

'Why?

He picked up his cigar, blew the smoke into the air then lowered his voice,

'There is a rumour that someone was smuggling stones.' He took another draw on the cigar and stared at me, 'Have you heard anything?' I paused; my hands suddenly felt clammy and my mouth went dry.

'No, I would come to you if I heard anything.' He tapped his head,

'Oh, something else.' He felt his pockets like he had misplaced something.

'An Arab trader who provides me with decent brandy and American cigars appears to have disappeared.' I stiffened and gulped as he glanced at me. The image of the Arab falling into the bush crossed my mind. I stuttered,

'Have you checked with his family?' shaking his head, he said,

'As far as I know, nobody knows of him.' He stared at me, 'You've gone pale, get more rest.'

Leaving the compound with a dry mouth; how could I warn Nkomo? The next day I went to the mine with my guys and informed everybody that they had a week's break from the mine duties. They took it well, with whoops and cheers. I waved my hands.

'Calm down, it's only a week.'

I checked everything in the tiny office that I had in a room off the canteen. Starting to put all the paperwork in order. A soldier who was helping me sort out the chaos mentioned that he studied to become an accountant but found it boring and joined the army instead. He was immediately promoted to office manager. When the shift ended and the miners, over twenty-five, lined up for a search, I spoke to them with the help of Ben that as of Monday the Congolese army was taking over, there were a few moans and curses.

By now the miners knew that my end-of-shift speech was not the same as the Congolese one. They didn't relish the thought of the rough treatment dished out by the soldiers for any infringements of the rules. As I watched the miners trudge to the waiting buses, Nkomo glanced at me and gave a short nod, I shook my head, hoping he got the message.

As I turned to walk away, I noticed that Rall and Pel were watching me, they observed me shaking my head to Nkomo. I stepped over to them and shook hands. Rall lit a cheroot. Pell grinned and said,

'Nkomo a friend of yours?'

Rall blew smoke in the air. Then with a fake puzzled expression said,

'Do you know why the Congolese are taking over next week?' Pel looked at him wide-eyed and grinning.

'They suspect one of the miners is smuggling stones.' Rall put a finger to his chin, 'But to who?'

They both stared with devious looks. Rall watched the ash fall off the end of his cheroot, 'Any idea boss man?' I shook my head a little too fast. My mouth was suddenly dry.

The next day I went to the mine, as usual, checked everything and everybody, then walking out of my office over to the mine, I saw Rall and Pel, dragging Nkomo over to the canteen.

I followed them and we all sat down, Nkomo's eyes were closed, his nose and mouth were bleeding, and his eyes were swollen. Rall looked at me, then smiling, poked Nkomo in the shoulder and said,

'This is the guy who has been passing over the stones,' Pel grinned,

'And guess whom he was passing them to? Rall quickly said,

'We can get a big bounty for this info.' They looked at each other and grinned. Rall gave a little nod,

'But it does not need to come to that if we come to some sort of arrangement, eh!' Pel stepped in front of him. His eyes narrowed as he said,

'What's your choice boss, a cash arrangement...or a one-way trip to the jungle.' They both lit up cheroots, and they had not stopped smiling since we met.

Rall stuck the foul-smelling cheroot between his brown teeth and then rubbed his hands.

'What's the offer boss man?' I coughed and waved the smoke away from my face.

No way would they have acted this way before they found my little secret. I tried to sound as if I was still in charge.

'Wait, I need to speak to Nkomo.' I bent down to Nkomo's shoulder and asked,

'What happened Nkomo?' He looked up and in a breaking voice,

'They came to my house last night with knives and said they would slit my kid's throats if I didn't tell them who I gave the stones to. At first, I told them it was a Belgium officer, but they didn't believe me, then they beat me. My wives screamed at them to stop, and shouted, 'Tell them what they want to know, or they will kill us all, so I told them that it was you who I gave the stones.' He dropped his head onto the table and started sobbing. Pel hissed,

'Come on, boss, what's your offer...make it big!' Still looking at Nkomo I muttered,

'What are you looking for?' Rall leaned forward; I could smell his sour breath.

'Five thousand.' There was a pause then Pel shoved him,

'No, ten thousand—every month or we talk.' He drew a finger across his throat and rasped,

'If not Nkomo will be a dead man lying in the jungle, and you will be shot or doing life in jail, and the rest of the Brits. will be thrown out of the Congo.' I held my hand up and interrupted.

'Wait, who have you told.' They looked at each other and laughed. 'Nobody! We don't want to wind up with a one-way trip to the jungle in the back of an army truck.' I smiled for the first time.

'Ok, good, I'll sort the money out, but first I'll take Nkomo back to his home in my jeep,

and get him cleaned up.' Pel shouted,

'Bring the money back.'

Rall rubbed his hands with excitement. I got Nkomo into my Jeep and drove out of the gates into the jungle. After a few moments, I pulled to the side of the road. 'Nkomo, listen carefully, go home, and tell your wives that last night when Rall and Pel beat you up and threatened the family, it did not happen, Understand? It did not happen.' He turned to me and spoke through a split bleeding mouth,

'OK boss.' I explained to him,

'Look, after the Congolese army has done their week's shift, we will talk about the stones' He nodded. Driving to the shanty town, he got out at one of the warrens of houses, pointing at a small tin-built house with a little yard at the side, I noticed kids playing at the front and two women hanging out washing.

Chapter 12

Driving to the barracks, my mind was racing as I sat on my bed, sinking my head into my quivering hands, what was I to do, this was serious. I could drive all night to the airport and get out of the country by tomorrow. What would happen to Nkomo and my British Soldiers? No, there must be another way.

I sat in the darkness for a few minutes trying to figure it out. I pulled the chest from under my bed, it had a change of uniform, some AK47 clips, and five grenades with timers attached, I shoved one grenade into my bag and set off to the mine. As I drove through the gates Rall and Pel came marching over, Pel blurted,

'Well, have you the money?' I nodded,

'It's all arranged, I have left a box with ten thousand American dollars with Raj at the beer hall, here is the key for the box,' *It was a spare key for my bedside cabinet.* Pel grabbed the key, and Rall said,

'Nice doing business boss.' They were giggling like little kids. I frowned,

'Wait, if you are going now won't that be a little suspicious?' Rall laughed,

'Who to? It's only Brits on duty and you are the boss.'

'Look, I said, why don't you take my jeep and I'll pick it up this evening from the bar?' Rall paused then grinned

'Sure boss, but we may want the jeep thrown in with the deal,' Pell laughed as he said,

'I've always wanted a Jeep.'

They were acting like they had hit the jackpot

I nodded,

'Ok guys, I can always get another Jeep. Get your stuff from the canteen and meet me in the parking area.' Still excited they walked briskly off to the canteen. I marched over to my Jeep, leaned over the back of the driver's seat and made sure the grenade was wedged tight. Winding the timer around to ten minutes then pressing the red button, a small blinking red light

58

came on, then I pulled an old pair of shorts over the grenade. Checking my watch. Rall and Pel came over with some bags and clothes. Pel jumped into the driver's seat.

Shuffling around uncomfortably in the seat.

'Hey boss, how do you adjust the seat?' I helped him move the seat forward and Rall got in. Playfully slapping Pel on the shoulder,

'Let's go partner.'

As they drove away, I noticed that the old shorts had fallen off. The grenade was exposed with the red-light blinking! I froze and stared at the tiny light.

The guards waved them through the gates, and they roared down the jungle path out of sight. I stood frozen on the spot. What if the timer stopped? What if the grenade failed to go off? What if, what if? The alarm vibrated on my wrist.

The explosion blew branches of trees into the air. The monkeys and birds were screeching in the jungle canopy, and a thin wisp of smoke rose above the canopy of trees in the distance.

A soldier came running over to me wide-eyed, and asked,

'What the hell was that?'

Trying to look ,surprised, I opened my hands

'They must have run over a mine.'

Archie and I with some others got into a jeep and drove out of the gates and along the jungle path, and came to a scene of carnage. Parts of a jeep were lying at the side of the bushes. A smoking wheel and part of the axle were on the other side of the road. Archie said,

'Look,' he pointed up into the trees.

Hanging from some branches was a badly burned body with both legs missing. Some guy shouted,

'Look here boss, there is another body in the bushes with his head missing, I guess he lost his head while driving,' the others laughed out loud. This was typical army humour; I managed a nervous grin.

We cleared the road and went back to the mine. Speaking to a Belgian officer, I said.

'I'll let the security police know about the incident this evening.' Driving back to the mine, I went into the canteen, Archie and Pete followed me in and sat. Pete held my hand, 'George, you're shaking, has that scene upset you?'

That evening I nervously approached the security police compound and found Bingo's office, he was with four other guys sitting by a table, drinking beer, and playing cards, rifles propped against the wall. Bingo looked up from the card table,

'I heard something about an explosion at the mine today.' I told him that two miners had got drunk and stolen my Jeep,

'It appears that they ran over a mine that the rebels had planted.' Bingo pulled a face,

'Rebels! What rebels?' One card player turned to Bingo,

'Yes boss, I heard that the rebels are going into the local villages, getting some of the younger guys to join them, and giving them shiny new rifles.' I could not believe my ears; I had just been let off the hook. Bingo gave orders to one of the card players.

'Step up patrols on the road to the mine,' he nodded then picked up a phone with a wind-up handle, put it to his ear, and talked in French. I caught some words like...rebelles!

I went back to my barracks and pulled out the chest from under my bed, I would have to hide the grenades and timers. If the place was searched, I'd have some explaining to do.

Saturday was busy for Murphy and the nuns, marrying some locals and divorcing others. But they seemed to be the Christian ones. The Congolese had their ceremonies which were more fun and colourful, with drums and dancing around in a circle,

Murphy called them heathens. Then there was the whipping, with some poor sod being tied to a post and whipped by Bingo, often the 'judge' would come shuffling up to the victim and read out the charge, he was a very old man, so skinny his ribs looked like short ladders under his skin.

With only a loincloth and a necklace of beads and teeth. John Lennon's glasses perched on the end of his nose and a judge's white wig at an angle on his head.

The locals believed that he possessed magic powers. He opened a tattered book the size of a large bible, then thumbed through a few pages. In a croaking, barely audible voice he read out the charge and the punishment,

closing the book, he turned around and shuffled back into the crowd.

Bingo whipped the unfortunate guy twice to the cheers of the crowd, he collapsed onto the dust as he was cut down. Then the drums would start, and the mob would start the shuffling and half-bent-over dancing with guns being fired into the air, making the monkeys scream and clouds of birds rise from the trees into the cloudless sky.

After watching Queenie, Rose's daughter, dancing with her boyfriend, a young security policeman. I left the crowd and strolled to Rose's house, a tin and wooden shanty-type dwelling. Banging on the door, it was opened by a Congolese soldier in Disney underpants. In the background, Rose was lying naked on a straw bed, and shouted,

'Come back in an hour George.'

As the door closed, I heard the sound of muffled laughter.

I made my way to the beer hall, past the mob dancing in a circle to drums. Archie and Pete were at a table with two other Brits. Archie excitedly said,

'Heard the news, there are rebels in this area. Guys who will shoot back.' He tapped his chin, 'I didn't sign up for this.' The others nodded,

'Come on boss, what is the situation?' I tried to put on a puzzled expression

'You guys know the same as me, any rebels are probably miles away' Pete raised his voice,

'Miles away!...they blew up the jeep with those two foremen less than a mile from the mine.' I couldn't tell them the truth on that one. I quickly said,

'Relax guys we are safe. Bingo is patrolling the roads and the army is doubling the guards around the compounds.' On Sunday, Franke the Belgian officer, who was the top man in charge of the military, summoned me to his compound. I sat down as he lit up a cigar, blowing smoke he asked,

'Any news on that trader? this is my last good cigar.'

The door opened and in strolled Bingo followed by a young Belgian guy. Bingo said,

'This is Rene, an investigator from Brazzaville.' Rene nodded to everyone, spread a paper bag on the table, and opened it up. There were bits of metal, a strip of clothing and a small piece of scorched white plastic. It was part of the timer from my grenade. Rene folded up the bag and put it on the floor, saying,

'I will take it back to forensics at police headquarters in Brazzaville, they may identify the type of mine;' I wiped my sweating hands on my shorts.

Driving back to the barracks, standing at the gates was Queenie, Rose's daughter, who said,

'George, my mother wants to see you.' Parking the jeep. We walked through the crowds in the square and to Rose's house. As I went in Rose was sitting at a table smoking weed. She was rolling another one, and said, 'Want some?'

'No thanks, Rose, that stuff doesn't agree with me.'

Queenie lit one up and sat at the back of the room reading a magazine. I said,

'Sorry for the intrusion this morning.'

Rose blew smoke into the air, laughed, and said,

'He is one of my ex-husbands, and Queenie's father—I think!' I sat close to her, whispering,

'Rose, I need to hide something for a little while.' She nodded,

'Sure, how big is it.'

Opening my hands a foot wide. She nodded again,

'Bring it over tonight.' I nodded in Queenie's direction, Rose glanced at Queenie, and said,

'She can keep her mouth shut.'

Going to the beer hall for a nightcap, the place was full of Brits. No guarding the mine for a week. Raj handed me a beer and put a finger in the air,

'I have something for you,' he handed over a large brown envelope. Without looking, I slipped it into my shorts, joined the Brits, and told them.

'Listen up guys, same time tomorrow, line up outside the compound for a one-mile jog with rifles and kit, same every day till we go back on duty at the mine...right!' *I was not the most popular guy at the table.*

I hurried back to the barracks to see what was in the envelope. Sitting on my bed I tore open the envelope. Out fell a French passport. The photo was not my photo, but it was me, the guy in the photo could have been my twin. My plan was becoming clear, I would take some of the stones, fly to London on my UK passport, and then fly to Antwerp on a French passport. Hopefully, sell the stones, and fly back to London on a French passport.

Spending one night in London, then back to Brazzaville on a UK passport, and on to the mine. So that if my UK passport was checked, it would show that I flew to London for a few days and nowhere else.

The next day I let Archie and Pete organize the Brits. I went into the shanty town for some money from the bank, cum post office, cum money changing office, then into the shanty town for shoes and trousers, a shirt and jacket and a carrier bag with a strong zip.

That night I waited till everyone was asleep, then left the compound, past one guard asleep, and the other saluted me, then plonked back on a chair.

The moon was like a huge white balloon,

dipping in and out of the trees, turning night into day, then just as quickly turning day into night as it dipped behind the trees.

I got into my jeep and drove out of the compound area, down the earth road for a couple of miles to a big tree with a narrow path running up the side.

Parking the jeep in the bushes I set off along the path. It was pitch black, but I had practised this walk many times. When I reached a tree stump at the side of the path, I measured out three paces, then with the short spade from the Jeep kit, I started to dig in the darkness. Six inches down I struck a wooden box. Like a blind man, I felt for the catch and opened the box, taking out two of the little bags and stuffed them into my short's pockets, closed the lid and pulled the earth over the top, patted it down and pulled the bushes back, then feeling my way along the path, back to the tree stump.

I found my jeep and drove slowly on my way back to the compound. Just at the end of the earth road, I was blinded by a searchlight, and a voice called out in French.

'Holt'—I pulled up and put my hands up. Two Congolese security policemen with torches that blinded me came up to the jeep. One stuck his rifle into my ribs, the other one recognized me and spoke to his colleague
in French, who lowered his rifle.

'What are you doing out here at this hour, do you know there are rebels in this area?'

I didn't answer. The other guy was looking into the back of the jeep. He held up the small shovel with fresh earth still sticking to it and looked at me for an answer. I had to think quickly.

'OK guys, the cleaners have a couple of cats that live in our barracks, we found one dead this morning, so as I could not sleep, I thought I would take it into the jungle and bury it and hoped it wouldn't be missed.' They both laughed, one of the policemen glanced at his colleague and said,

'OK…but wait, we were told to search everybody.'

I started up the jeep and with a nervous laugh said, 'You think I am hiding another cat?' They laughed as I drove off.

It was a cool night, but I was sweating.

Back at the barracks, I put the bags under my bed, I had a nightmare thinking if they had searched me and found the stones. My luck was holding out.

The next morning the Brits were lined up for inspection. Parked in the square were two army trucks full of Congolese soldiers going to take our place at the mine. I took Archie to one side, and said, 'Archie, I am going to London on a bit of business, look after things here, if any of the Brits ask why I am not here, say I've gone to Brazzaville for a meeting.' Archie stared at me with a blank look...'You *are* coming back?'

Putting my hand on his shoulder I smiled, 'God willing Archie, God willing.'

I made my way to Maya-Maya airport at Brazzaville and booked a room to shower, change, and get a good night's rest. Early the next morning I flew directly to London.

Going through customs in London I held declare. At the end of the lobby, a young customs officer leaned against the wall and checked his watch, he was counting the minutes to the end of his long shift. I held a long breath and walked straight through like a man late for an appointment, to the door marked—Exit.

Chapter 13

Booking into a hotel at the airport I discovered that the next flight to Antwerp was tomorrow evening. I showered and changed, drenched myself in the aftershave on the bathroom shelf, and went to the crowded bar. Two black-label Johnnie Walker whiskies later, I felt back in civilisation. no guys with guns, no stifling heat, no bush meat dinners.

Sitting at the bar holding a whisky, I noticed a young lady sitting at the bar looking over. She was in her twenties, wearing a flowery catsuit, auburn hair and a lovely smile that made her eyes crinkle. I held up my glass and smiled back. She strolled over, sat on the next stool, and purred,

'Mind if I join you?' She smiled again showing a gold tooth, 'I've been stood up by my ex-boyfriend, he was supposed to meet me for a romantic dinner.' She grinned, 'I think his wife suspects something,' She stuck a well-manicured hand out.

'My name is Magda.' I smiled and shook her hand.

'And my name is Santa Claus. What would you like to drink Magda?' She glanced at my glass and then quickly replied…'I'll have what you are having.' *This began to sound like a Humphrey Bogart movie.*

Talking, I found her easy to talk to, an intelligent girl who could hold a serious conversation, and that always pressed my buttons. Two hours later we were both very drunk when I muttered,

'OK honey, I have a busy day tomorrow, I am off to bed.'

She slid off her stool, flung her arms around my neck, and said,

'I'll have to stay with you tonight, I am too drunk to drive home, and I haven't got any money for a room.' She kind of answered the question. I mumbled,

'Sure, why not!'

We struggled to make it to the lift. It took me several tries to get the key in the door.

I struggled to get my clothes off. Feeling sick, I staggered into the bathroom to see Magda, sitting on the toilet, naked, with her head in her hands and moaning,

'I don't feel well!'

The wash basin was perfect for a guy over six feet tall. I got back into bed and passed out. About three hours later Magda was shaking me and crying,

'Santa, help me, I am ill, take me to the toilet.' I swung my legs out of the side of the bed, everything was spinning in my head.

Magda climbed onto my back with her arms around my chest and her legs wrapped around my waist. I staggered upright and started to shuffle around the bed towards the bathroom when I felt something warm spreading down my lower back and my legs, it was like lava...and stank!

She was crying, 'Sorry, sorry.' I made it to the shower and we got in. Turned on the shower to warm and grabbed a loafer to wash Magda's bum and legs, when she was clean, I said,

'Now it's your turn.' Turning around, she washed the shit off.

I then hugged her, smiled weakly, and said,

'How much more romantic can this get.' She looked down and gave a weak smile.

In the morning we dressed and went down to a beautiful breakfast. Magda didn't speak about last night; I felt her embarrassment. After breakfast, it was,

'Goodbye Magda, I have a lot of work to do.' I kissed her goodbye, and went back upstairs, put the do not disturb notice on the door, checked my bag, got into bed, and went to sleep instantly.

It was dark when I awoke. Shadows of car lights crossed the ceiling. I had forgotten to close the drapes. My watch showed there were two hours until my flight. I took a long hot shower and a slow shave. Paying the bill and got the hotel receptionist to get me a taxi to the airport.

In the duty-free, I bought a bottle of the aftershave Joop my favourite...I had almost forgotten how to smell nice!

Chapter 14

After a short flight, I landed at Antwerp airport. I climbed into a yellow taxi covered in signs. handing the driver a fifty-dollar note and saying,

'Take me to a hotel, the closest to the diamond centre.' The driver was a young, bearded Arab guy who glanced at my bag,

'Buying or selling sir,'

I said the first thing that came into my head,

'Neither, I am here to fix a telephone system.'

I was let off at a small hotel, that looked more like a bed and breakfast. I went in to book a room. The teenager at the reception desk was pale-faced with a receding hairline and the straggly beginnings of a beard. Sitting on a stool reading a magazine and smoking a cigarette, he shoved the magazine under the desk and put the cigarette into a tin ashtray as I approached.

'You will have to leave your passport sir.'

I queried, 'Why?'

He stared at me as if I had asked a stupid question.

'I am sorry sir; I don't make the rules.' I opened my bag and started to pull out my French passport...oops. Then handed my British one over. He glanced at the photo then nodded, 'Thanks.' Handing me a key attached to a plastic card with a number and pointing to the stairs.

'One flight up, sorry, the lift is out of order.' As I picked up the key and turned away, he pulled out the magazine and picked up the cigarette. The room was cosy with a small ensuite bathroom, tea-making stuff, and a roll of chocolate biscuits. The bed felt soft when I fell into it and was asleep in minutes.

The next morning, I awoke to somebody knocking on the door, followed by a ...'Breakfast ends in fifteen minutes, sir.' I had slept in longer than I wanted.

Dressing quickly, I grabbed my bag and went downstairs. After some good coffee and a croissant, I left and got directions from an old guy selling newspapers outside the door.

A taxi found the address.

A long cobbled, dimly lit street. On the old part of town, with even darker streets leading off it. I found the house that had a faded lopsided sign above the door,

Cohen Bro. Diamond Cutters, trade only. There was a smell of blocked drains. Two rats scuttled across the cobbles and into a hole in the wall. I knocked on the heavy timber door, no answer, I knocked louder, and a little post box at eye level opened, and a voice spoke in French. Before the voice finished speaking,

'Sorry, 'I don't speak French.'

There was a pause then an English voice said,

'Just a moment sir.' A moment later the door creaked open several inches, and an old Jew wearing an oversized skull cap and a shawl over his head and shoulders, glared at me.

'What do you want?' Peering into the crack I said,

'I would like some advice.' In the gloom, I saw that he was grinning when he said,

'You have come to the wrong door; you need the citizen's advice bureau,' he replied.

He broke into a cackle and then coughed; a younger guy stepped in front of him.

The door opened, and a condescending voice said,

'Forgive him, sir, what do you need advice for?'

Holding my bag up I said,

'I have an uncut stone.' Before I could say anything else, the door swung open. He took my arm, pulled me in and shut the door. His mouth curled into a grin.

'You have come to the right place, sir.'

He led me along a narrow lobby and into a brightly lit room with a dozen or so men and boys all wearing skullcaps and some with shawls over their shoulders, sitting at what looked like sewing machines. He led me through the room to another room and knocked. A muffled voice shouted,

'Come.' We entered a smoke-filled room with three older men sitting on a huge sofa that had seen better days, with another guy sitting at a long table reading a newspaper with a magnifying glass.

The older guy with a white beard and pigtails hanging from his skull cap had a shawl around his shoulders and was eating a kind of thick soup. Glancing at me, the old man grunted and spoke in Yiddish. The guy sitting next to him looked at me and said,

'Moshe asked, what have you got to show me.'

I had a single stone in a side pocket and put it on the table, everyone leaned over to the table. The guy with the newspaper folded it up, and the old man with the beard stopped eating and leaned over, adjusting his glasses. The younger one took an eyeglass from his coat and shouted to the next room.

'Danny, Come,' a door opened and in walked Danny Cohen. A tall smartly dressed guy with a skull cap and black thick-rimmed glasses. He sounded excited as he spread his arms out.

'What have you got to show us?'

He spoke with a slight American accent; the younger Jew spoke to him in Yiddish as he handed him the stone. The room had an air of expectation, as everyone stared in silence.

Danny took out an eyeglass and studied the stone, then called to a diamond cutter from the other room to bring a lamp. Nothing was said as Danny examined it through the lamp and then handed it to the cutter. He looked at it through the lamp and nodded. Danny sat next to me.

'It is a very rough stone, not worth a lot.' The Jews sitting on the sofa all shook their heads like nodding dolls. I paused, I didn't know what to expect, but this wasn't it. I stood and spoke.

'Ok, I'll try somewhere else.' I reached for the stone,

'Wait, wait.' Danny held on to the stone, saying with a hint of urgency,

'Look, you have come a long way, we will offer you something for your trouble.' He passed the stone to the old man eating the soup. Putting the spoon down and Danny passed him an eye-glass, Danny uttered,

'This is my grandfather, Moshe...' Moshe nodded with a straight face, picked up an eyeglass and looked at the stone again, then spoke to Danny in Yiddish. Danny looked with a half-smile and said,

'How much do you want,' I replied,

'Danny, you know by now that I don't have a clue about the value of the stones,' he smiled and nodded as if to agree. I raised my voice,

'But there is a whole load of diamond dealers in this town who will be happy to tell me its value, so I'll just take my stone and go.' He grabbed my arm, and with a hint of mild panic said,

'Wait, wait George Let' not be so hasty, have some coffee.' He called out to a young boy in the background. shaking his hand loose I said,

'So, you give me the proper price, or I'll try elsewhere, and you will lose the business.'

The boy came with the coffee. Danny spoke with Moshe who had finished his soup and was wiping his beard, then whispered to Danny. Danny said,

'My grandfather is asking if could there be any more stones from this source?' Everybody sitting around the table leaned forward in silence. I smiled at Moshe, opened my arms, and raised my voice,

'Enough to fill a chest!' Everyone sat back in their seats and started chattering.

Moshe took the stone and looked at it again with his eyeglass. He spoke to Danny who said,

'Moshe says he will give you thirty thousand dollars...' I choked on my coffee, was I hearing things? My eyes watered. I squeezed my cup in both hands as I stuttered.

'Did your grandfather say — thirty thousand?'

Danny paused then sounding irritated said,

'OK thirty-three thousand...but that's it.' I put my coffee cup down, reached over the table shook Moshe's hand, and said,

'You drive a hard bargain, sir.'—*I would have accepted a tenth of that price!*

Moshe called out to a guy who was in the background, who left the room and returned five minutes later carrying a large wooden box and gave it to Danny, who pulled out wads of high-value American dollars. *I still couldn't believe the stones were worth that much, I would have been happy with a thousand bucks.*

Watched by the silent crowd he counted thirty-three thousand dollars, put them in a plastic shopping bag and handed it to me. Danny asked,

'What else have you got?' I paused, picked up my coffee and took a long slow drink. Everyone was staring at me. I heard somebody slam a fist onto the table.

Danny whispered

'Hurry up and finish your bloody coffee, you are upsetting my grandfather.'

I reached into my pocket and pulled another three stones out. There was the scraping of chairs being pushed back on the wooden floor as everyone stood and leaned over the table.

Danny walked around the table and helped Moshe to his feet, who stared at the stones glinting on the wood, then muttered in English,

'Oi vey.' More already.'

Nearly everyone took a turn looking at the stones through an eyeglass, like some kind of religious ceremony. We finished the session with me having a bag with four hundred and thirty-three thousand dollars, Danny remarked, 'So much money.' I tried to appear calm as I asked,

'Is there a bank where I can put this for a little while?' Danny nodded,

'Come with me,' he said goodbye to his grandfather Moshe and his father, Isaac. The whole room waved me goodbye, like excited children.

Danny walked me through the narrow, cobbled streets to a taxi rank. I was nervous, I had only met these guys and now I am walking with them carrying a load of cash. looking over my shoulder more than once I got into the taxi with Danny. Giving the taxi driver instructions, off we went. Danny leaned back on the seat, and said,

'Do you know George, that a guy was knifed to death for a dozen francs and a pair of shoes,' he was quiet for a moment, then laughed, 'Don't worry, Moshe is a good judge of people, and he told me, you are a good man.'

We got out at a bank and went inside with the bag. At the counter, Danny spoke to the manager whom he seemed to know well, and he showed us to a small room.
Danny explained that I needed a haven
for my money, 'No problem, sir,' the manager said,

'We have a strong room where you can rent a strongbox, or you can open an account,' I hesitated, 'Thanks, I would like to open an account. Picking up an internal phone he spoke in French, a moment later a knock on the door and a young woman came in with a sheaf of papers, she sat with me and Danny, and five minutes later I was a customer. Another girl came in, and it took them almost half an hour to count and tie up the money, place it in a metal box and leave. The manager was a well-dressed young guy who talked about stock and shares and other boring stuff. He grinned as he told me he was reprimanded for having an affair with the wife of a customer.

'Normally it was a sacking offence, but the chairman of the bank was beaten into second place in a golfing tournament by the customer who cheated to win.' We all laughed. I kept back the thirty-three thousand and stuffed it in my bag.

Danny was in a buoyant mood, he hadn't stopped grinning since we left the shop,

'We will go for coffee and discuss some matters, then if you pick up your stuff from your hotel you are coming to my home as my guest,' I nodded,

'Ok, sounds good.' *I had the feeling of being soft-soaped, but who's complaining?*

I went upstairs to my room, and Danny waited downstairs at the desk, I reached under the bed and pulled out a bag containing the last stone, it was a stone with a dazzling blue tint. Shoving it in my pocket I went downstairs. The guy in the reception shoved a magazine under the desk as I said,

'How much do I owe?' the teenager scowled at me,

'You said two days and now you are leaving after one, I must charge you a fee,' his eyes narrowed as he grinned, he was holding my passport and nodding, I said,

'Ok, I understand,' I paid, got my passport and we left.

We found a taxi outside the hotel, and Danny spoke in French to the driver.

Closing his eyes as he leaned back, and said, 'My chateau is on the outskirts of Antwerp.' Driving out of town, then another long trip through the never-ending farmland and tree-lined countryside.

We left the motorway and drove along a single gravel country road, stopping at a large Chateau with big iron gates, surrounded by farmland.

We got out and Danny strode to a huge stone pillar at the side of the gates, opening a small wooden box, hanging at eye level, he pressed a switch, and the big iron gates started to slowly swing open. Walking up a short driveway to the door of the chateau. A huge black American Cadillac Eldorado was parked outside the door. Danny opened the carved oak door,

'Come on in George,' he led me into a kitchen- cum dining room, it all looked very French, but dated, an old woman was sitting in a huge rocking chair, Knitting, with a cat on her lap, she looked up and nodded then returned to her Knitting. Danny sat me down at the long dining table,

'First coffee, then I'll show you your room.' He walked through a side door and moments later returned with two cups of coffee, and said, 'Meet my lovely wife, Madam Celine,' he shouted out 'Celine! Come and meet our guest.' A door at the end of the room opened and in walked a vision of beauty! Black waived hair, huge brown eyes, perfect mouth, and white teeth.

Once in a while you will meet a naturally beautiful woman, this was such a time. She wore no make-up, the kind of beauty that didn't need it. She reached over with slender outstretched hands, I shook her hand and noticed well-manicured nails and a diamond ring the size of a peanut.

'Welcome to our humble Chateau,'
she spoke Oxford English with a slight French accent and smiled, showing perfect teeth. We finished the coffee, and then Danny took me upstairs, into a huge room with an enormous bed, and a French baroque-style carved bedhead. Pointing to a door.

'There is a shower room next door, I'll send you up a change of clothes,' he stood back and looked me up and down then nodded, 'Yes, we are the same height and build.'

I started to unpack when the bedroom door opened and a young black maid came in with a pile of clothes and a pair of shoes. She put them on the bed, said something in French, paused for a moment as if waiting for a reply, shook her head and left. A phone rang. It took me a moment or two to find it.' Celine's voice purred, in English with a sexy French accent.

'George, dinner in one hour, Ok?

I mumbled,

'Yes, one hour is fine.'

Showered in the biggest shower cubicle that I have ever seen, four people could have comfortably fitted in. Then dressing in Danny's clothes, a little too big, but they were good quality, even the shoes were polished. Checking my bag, I put the last stone in a little side pocket. I had a feeling about this stone, it was bigger than the others with a blue tinge.

Strolled downstairs, I sat at a beautifully laid out table, with coloured candles that gave the room a relaxed vibe, two maids served the soup, then the main dish. Chicken in a white wine sauce. Over the apple pie and ice cream, the conversation was flowing, Celine was nonstop,

'Where did I come from? How long was I in the diamond business?' Danny was silent but listening to every word. We finished the meal and Danny proclaimed with pride,

'I have some Cuban cigars,' I shook my head,

'No thanks,'

Danny sounded disappointed when he said,

'Do you mind if I have one?' before I could reply, he opened a large wooden cigar box and took one out, cut off the end and after sniffing it, feeling it, staring at it for a moment he stuck it in his mouth and lit up. I felt like it was the equivalent of the Japanese tea ceremony. Celine purred,

'Would you like a brandy?'

I shook my head,

'Thanks no, but do you have a Scottish whisky?' those amazing eyes widened,

'Yes of course!' She smiled, 'Any special brand?'

Trying to sound like I knew my whiskies.

'Yes, I prefer a Johnnie Walker black label...if you have one?

Celine called a maid in and spoke to her in French, minutes later the maid appeared with a tray, containing a lead crystal glass, a dish with ice cubes and a bottle of whisky.

I sat at one side of the table sipping my whisky with Danny on the other side blowing smoke to the ceiling. He put the cigar into a large marble ashtray, and said,

'Down to business.

You said you have more stones to sell?'

'Yes Danny, just one more on this trip, but I think you will like this one, it has a blue tint and is larger than the others.'

Danny stiffened, slowly picked up his cigar and without making eye contact muttered,

'A blue tint?' He stood and went to the phone sitting on a side table. Speaking in Yiddish for three minutes, then came and sat down, picked up his glass he raised his voice.

'A toast to you my friend,' I stood up, with a glow of good whisky inside me, I said,

'And a toast to you, Celine, Moshe and Isaac, and the Cohen brothers, cheers...and now a trip to bed, see you all in the morning.'

Holding onto the Bannister as I had had a few of the famous black labels. As I opened the bedroom door it creaked a little. I undressed and took a shower to sober up, then into that huge soft bed with silk sheets and giant white pillows. I stretched out and went to sleep.

I awoke to the door creaking open. Leaning up I called out,

'Who's there?' By the light of a full moon shining through the huge windows, stood Celine, naked, and with a smile whispered, 'Mind if I join you?' I stammered...

'But Danny! She put a finger to my lips and said,

'I've put a little something in Danny's nightcap.' She slid into those silk sheets, as we locked bodies. I mumbled,

'Wait, I feel guilty, Danny has treated me well.'

She looked at me with those piercing brown eyes in the moonlight and muttered,

'Danny has been having an affair with one of my friends for years, he is in love with her and would divorce me if he could, but his father and Moshe told him, no, so don't feel guilty besides, Danny asked me to make a fuss of you,' she smiled, 'So here I am!' she kissed me on my neck, my face, my lips, the smell of her expensive perfume and that woman was overwhelming.

We got down to the business in hand for the next two hours, stopping for a break. I could not keep up with her...Literally. We were both covered in sweat as Celine ran her hands over my stomach and remarked,

'What is this?' She turned me over to the moonlight shining through the huge window. Putting her hand on my stomach, peering down, and remarking,

'You have a small mole on your hip, in the shape of a heart, that's unusual.'

We spent another half hour pleasing each other, and then I closed my eyes and collapsed onto the pillow, I felt a kiss on my nose and heard a door creaking shut.

In the morning, rising early, I could still
smell Celine's perfume, I showered and dressed, put the blue stone in my pocket and took my bag downstairs, Danny was waiting, He made coffee and we sat, Danny yawned,

'I was knocked out last night, did you sleep well.' I grinned 'Yes, apart from a few bangs.' He looked puzzled and said,

'Did you enjoy the meal?' He smiled; 'I know you enjoyed the whisky.'

We finished our coffee and went out into the driveway.

'You'll say goodbye to Celine for me?' I said, Danny looked a little puzzled as he looked at his watch.

'Celine is normally up at this hour, she may be exhausted from cooking and setting up the meal.'

I nodded in agreement.

A taxi was waiting outside the big iron gates, we got in and Danny told the driver in French where we wanted to go, I took a last look at the chateau and saw a figure at a window waving.

Danny spoke non-stop on the long journey back to Antwerp, about future deals, how his grandfather, Moshe, wanted the whole family to move to Jerusalem in Israel to start a diamond-cutting business there, Danny shook his head, saying ,

'Maybe in a few years.'

We arrived at the street just down from the shop, walking up the cobbles to the shop door, Danny gave a coded knock on the door. Minutes later I was sitting at the table with Danny, Moshe, and Isaac his father said, 'Well, well, what have you got to show us,'

I thought that I would play games.

'Coffee first,' I ventured. Moshe and Danny swore together and shouted for coffee.

I sat back in the chair; Moshe was swearing in French. Danny went to the kitchen and hurried back with the coffee putting it in front of me and said,

'Drink it before it gets cold.'

They sat in silence while I slowly drank my coffee.

Moshe shuffled his feet and wiped his brow, finally putting my cup on the table a hand snatched it away.

I pulled out the blue stone and put it on the table, everyone leaned over the table as if the room had tilted. Danny handed the stone to Moshe, who peered at the stone with his eyeglasses, he put the glasses and the stone on the table and spoke to Danny in Yiddish, Danny smiled, and said,

'Moshe knows where this stone comes from,' Moshe nodded and gave a sly smile, Danny said that he had told him,

'There is one mine that produces a blue diamond...Mbuji-Mayi in the Congo.'

Moshe picked up the eyeglasses and looked at the stone again, he spoke to Danny who turned to me,

'Moshe said he must have this stone!' I nodded,

'Make me an offer?'

He slapped my shoulder,

'Let's have more coffee, we have a few calls to make,' Danny spoke into the phone then handed the phone to his father who spoke for two minutes then handed the phone to Moshe who spoke for a minute and then started shouting and cursing down the phone, he calmed down and spoke again for another three minutes, putting the phone down and nodding. Everyone sat and started talking. I saw that Moshe was clutching the blue stone.

After another coffee and a salt beef sandwich later, the door opened, and two men came in. They both had long beards and pigtails hanging down their cheeks from big felt hats with wide brims and were dressed all in black. There was a round of shaking hands, and then Moshe hand-ed the blue stone to the elder man who studied it for a few moments, he then turned to me and spoke in an American accent. 'How much my friend?' I told him 'That I was going to do the rounds to get the best offer, but the Cohen family have been generous to me so I will give them first refusal.' The man spoke in Yiddish with the others, then took out a calculator and huddled over the table with everybody talking.

He straightened up and stared at me for a moment, everybody went silent as he said,

'One offer, my friend.' He sucked in a breath.—'Three hundred thousand.' There was silence as everybody held their breath. Danny was clasping his hands as if in prayer. Moshe had his eyes closed. Isaac was staring at the ceiling. There was silence in the room, with only the ticking of the clock on the wall...I nodded my head.

'Ok, three hundred thousand it is.' The room erupted, Danny slapped my back, Moshe and Danny's father hugged me, and the guy who served the coffee patted me on the back.

The two guys in black suits went out of the room and came back in less than ten minutes with a big leather case, one guy took out bundles of American dollars, wrapped in plastic bags, and each bundle had five thousand dollars with a bank stamp on it. He put sixty bundles into my canvas shopping bag. The two men in black picked up the leather suitcase and left

Moshe was holding onto the blue stone. I said my goodbyes to everyone then Danny took me in a taxi to the same bank that I had been to before. Danny called the young manager, and we all went into a side room. Danny explained that I needed a haven for the three hundred thousand dollars. The manager suggested, putting it into the account with the other four hundred thousand, I agreed, and the manager picked up a phone and spoke in French, moments later two girls came in with a metal box and a handful of paperwork, opened my shopping bag and started to take out the bundles of dollars to count.

The manager left and a few minutes later came back with three coffees on a tray with sugar and a jug of cream. I signed the papers and was given a receipt with my photograph and a five-digit line with the number five at the end, but no bank details or contact number.

After some light talk about the terrible state of the world, the girls put the money into the metal box and left. I said my goodbyes to Danny I caught a taxi to Antwerp Airport.

Chapter 15

There was a flight to London in two hours, I used my French passport.

Taking the walk-through exit channel in customs unhindered and boarded the plane. A short flight and I was at the London airport an hour and a half later. I waited till the crowd all converged at the customs, with only two customs officers on duty and at the end of their long shift I was waved through, it was a trick that I learned from Danny. As I went through there was a noise at the customs point, a drunk woman was demanding to be searched! I walked away shaking my head. Booking into the airport hotel, the receptionist booked me in on the computer and said,

'Back again with us Mr. Stephen.'
Giving me a well-rehearsed smile...

I showered and changed, then down to the bar, the same bar where I had met Magda.

Downing a couple of Johnnie Walkers, I got talking to a guy who had just left the army, he was stationed in the Netherlands and over a drink told me that he was an ex-tank commander and, before he left the army, he was told that a guy in his position and experience would walk into a top job back in the UK. He smirked as he told me that he applied for twenty-five positions that he thought he could handle, and he received four letters back, he grinned as he said,

'Basically, who needs a tank commander in an insurance office.' We both laughed.

Another couple of Mr Walker's best, then it was off to bed to dream of that successful day.

The next day at nine-thirty prompt I was in the queue to board the flight to Maya–Maya the Brazzaville airport in the Congo, then onto a train, a bus, and a taxi and I was back 'home' late at night. I had forgotten the smells, humidity, mosquitoes, and jungle noises. There were Congolese soldiers at every place, smoking and some drinking cans of beer, uneducated village guys in uniforms. Home sweet home.

In the morning I presented myself to the British soldiers before they set off in their jeeps. I spoke with Archie and Pete, who shook my hand like a long-lost friend and hugged me. Telling them,

'I have got some money for you guys.'

Their eyes lit up, Archie rubbed his hands,

'How much, how much?' I turned to Pete and said,

'A thousand each.' A moment later they set off patting each other on the back.

I walked to the Belgian officer's compound and entered his office he was sitting studying reports. Looking up, he said,

'Where the hell have you been,' looking surprised I asked, 'Why?' he went on, 'When the Congolese took over the guarding at the mine, there was a couple of fights broke out between the miners and the army, and a miner was shot in the leg, so the rest of the miners and other workers stopped work. I sent Bingo and the security police to the mine with crates of beer, and they took over the shift from the army, who left. The miners spent the rest of the day sitting in the canteen getting drunk and talking about compensation for the shot miner. Bingo promised a big party on Saturday, with free beer for the miners. They got on the buses in a better mood, so, I decided to send in your Brits for the rest of the week to calm things down. Then Bingo came to my office and asked who was going to pay for the free beer?' He paused and tapped the desk, 'Oh, and by the way, there is an American film crew arriving here tomorrow, you have been put in charge of their security. Opening my mouth to speak, He quickly said, 'Orders from Brazzaville.'

Chapter 16

Saying goodbye, I left, took a spare jeep, and drove to the shanty town, I wanted to check on the money being paid into the Brits and my account, I was about to leave the post office, come bank when the manager walked over to me with a handful of small parcels and letters. He told me that the guy who normally takes the letters to the compounds has been sick for a couple of days,

'Would you mind handing them over?'

'Sure.' I nodded as I took the mail.

I drove back to the Brit's compound. A local that I knew from the bar was standing at the gate speaking to one of the Brit guards. Leaning out of my seat, I said,

'Hi buddy, I'll give you two dollars to deliver these letters and parcels.' Placing them one at a time into his arms, I noticed a letter was addressed to the Belgian officer, it was from the police headquarters in Brazzaville and marked forensics, I put that letter in my pocket, then gave the guy a couple of dollars and off he went.

I spoke to the British guards for a couple of minutes, then went inside and sat on my bed, ripped open the letter, it was in French, but I caught the words, plastic timer, and British army. Jeez, I had forgotten that meeting with the cop from Brazzaville who told us that he was going to send some bits from the explosion to the office of forensics in Brazzaville, this letter was their findings. Whom could I trust to translate the letter...? Rose! Trudging over the concrete and tarmac square, and up an unlit side path to Rose's house. Rose opened the door and hugged me, kissing my cheek, her breath was a cross between stale beer and an out-of-date curry,

'Come in and I'll make us a coffee.' Sitting at her bamboo table, I handed her the letter, and out of the folds of her dress tunic, she put on a pair of battered glasses, held together with tape.

I drank my coffee in silence, while she translated French into English, and then she told me, the letter said, 'That a mine did not cause the explosion, it was a British army grenade with a timer. Then it goes on to say, look closer to home for the killer. Someone who had a reason to want them dead!' I took a deep breath, *suppose this had reached the Belgian Officer or Bingo, the guy in charge of the Congolese security police, who would love to have me out of the way.*

My luck was holding out, but for how much longer? I thanked Rose, took the letter, and left. Rose called to me as I left,

'Queenie is getting married on Saturday, don't miss it.'

A local was leaning against the wall of a house smoking, I borrowed a match and burned the letter, I was hoping everybody had forgotten the meeting, and Rose would keep her mouth shut.

That evening I met Archie and Pete in the beer hall, we sat in a corner with some beers,

'Thanks, guys, for looking after things while I was away, and I have some money for you both,' Pete said, 'Where did you get money from?' I couldn't tell them of my trips to Antwerp, the less they knew the safer for all.

'I got a bonus from Brazzaville; they are pleased with the reports that they are receiving.' Archie rubbed his hands,

'How much?'

'A thousand each.' I said,

'Wow,' Archie's eyes lit up, and Pete gave a sly smile. I had twenty thousand dollars in my bag, but I could not give them that in case they went mental and wanted to know where the money came from.

The next day a couple of large furniture vans and a dust-covered car pulled up in the compound square. Four American guys and a woman were introduced to me by the Belgian,

'George, let me introduce you to the famous American show host — Alice Bentley.'

In my head, I heard a roll of drums. We shook hands, and the Belgian turned to the woman.

'George will look after you and the crew, anything you need to know, just ask him. He turned quickly away; I whispered in his direction.

'Thanks, Dick head.' Alice was a short middle-aged plump lady, with neat hair and little make-up, not beautiful but certainly good-looking. She looked like a woman whom you didn't mess with. Alice gave a fake smile and in a strong American accent said,

'I need you to organize a crowd for some action shots.'

I had a pen and paper at the ready, and asked,

'Ok, how many? And what for?' Alice explained,

'For a riot scene. Mobutu has taken over the Congolese government; he's had the prime minister Patrice Lumumba assassinated.' She lit a cigarette, blowing smoke into the still air and muttered, 'Whomever he was.' The American crew was busy making placards...

Down with Mobutu, in English, I said,

'Alice, the people here don't understand English, everything is in French in this country.'

She looked puzzled, flicking a half-smoked cigarette and in a slow drawl, spat out,

'I don't give a rat's ass what god-forsaken language they speak in this shithole, this is for my American viewers.'

I rounded up a dozen Congolese soldiers who were eager to earn twenty francs for twenty minutes of work. One of the crew signalled them to march towards him, waving the placards and waving their arms. Cameras rolled for a minute then the sound man shouted,

'Cut! That's a wrap. The Congolese soldiers continued to shout and wave the placards till the guy with a bundle of francs appeared, the placards were dropped on the ground raising clouds of dust. The soldiers lined up for the pay and then were seen heading towards the bar.

'Where can I get a decent drink in this steaming dump?' Alice asked. I led her and the crew down to the beer hall, it was full of the soldiers that they had just paid. She looked around in amazement,

'Jeez! this is like the wild west.' We went to the bar, and Raj put on his best smile,

'What can I get you, madam!'

She lit a cigarette, then with a Mae West impersonation, 'A dry Martini stirred not shaken.' Raj burst out laughing, he called out to some of the soldiers at the nearest table and spoke in French. As the soldiers laughed out loud. She turned to me,

'What's so fucking funny? Has nobody heard of cocktails in this God-forsaken country?'

Raj served up beers and whisky to the crew, and Alice settled for a whisky sour.

The front door swung open and in swaggered Bingo, escorted by two Congolese security cops, he came over and I introduced Alice, she shook his hand and said,

'And who are you?' Bingo grinned,

'I am the law in this town!' Alice smiled,

'You speak perfect English.' Bingo ordered a beer and beaming, asked, 'What would the beautiful lady like to drink,' she smiled at Bingo,

'Hey, I like this guy!'

'I must go now,' I said, 'You are all staying at the Belgian officer's compound, it is all arranged, see you later.' Alice called me as I stepped out the door. She lowered her voice,

'I must do a couple of interviews in the morning, then we are out of this fleapit.'

Driving back to the barracks, I had a bag with over twenty thousand dollars under my bed, I thought if I could recover the bags of stones from my hiding spot in the jungle, and get them to Antwerp, I'd be out of here for good. No more bush meat food. No more heat and mosquitos. No more diseases that the world had yet to find a name for.

Chapter 17

It was after midnight when I awoke to someone firing a rifle in the square. Slipping into my shorts I went out to the square, in the darkness half a dozen drunk soldiers were arguing, shoving each other around and generally making a noise. I decided to let the security police and Bingo sort this one out. I walked over to Bingo's compound, and the guard let me in. Finding Bingo's room I knocked, but no answer. Opening the door, I stepped in. In the half-light, Alice was lying in bed naked next to Bingo, who was snoring. I smiled and quietly closed the door.

The next morning, I saw the Brits off to the mines on the jeeps and then went to the square. The American crew was there, but no Alice! Five minutes later a jeep with Bingo and Alice rolled up, Alice got out, looking the worse for wear and told the crew,

'Bingo kindly picked me up from the Belgian officer's compound.' Bingo winked as he drove away. The American crew nodded to each other and grinned. Alice lit a cigarette and said,

'George, can you get me a beer, my throat is kind of dry.'

The rest of the morning was doing interviews and filming the locals, and the jungle. Even the monkeys got into the act. Then they packed the cameras and other gear into the vans. Alice came over and gave me her card, 'If you're ever in LA look me up.'

I nodded, 'Thanks, Alice, and I don't snore!' She winked and blew a kiss. Ten minutes later they were all gone in a cloud of dust.

That Saturday was special, Rose's daughter Queenie was to wed her security man boyfriend. But Rose told me that the previous night they had a big bust-up, so it was fifty-fifty if there was going to be a wedding. Rose winked,

'But George, we can still have the after-wedding booze-up?'

Murphy and his nuns made their way up the road, throwing holy water over the faithful, and anyone else that put a few francs in the nun's bowls. Murphy nodded to me as he passed.

I was standing with a couple of Brits when Queenie and the groom appeared. Murphy droned,

'If anyone has good reason, that this couple should not be joined in holy matrimony, let them speak now or forever hold their peace.' Over a dozen voices shouted out, and one of the security men shouted,

'He is already married.'

The crowd broke out into laughter. Murphy went on,

'Do you Asre, take this woman to be your lawful wedded wife.' Asre cleared his throat,

'Non,' Murphy ignored him and turned to Queenie, before he said anything Queenie shouted, 'Non,' then marched off into the cheering crowd, Asre was left with Murphy, who said,

'I now pronounce you man and wife; you may kiss the bride.' Murphy whispered,

'If you can find her.'

A poor soul was dragged across the square by two security men, tied to the post. This was entertainment for the crowd, and then the 'judge' shuffled through the mob. John Lennon glasses on the end of his nose, and a judge's white wig on his bald head. He opened a book as the crowd hushed, and in a croaky voice shouted,

'This man stole a chicken from another man's wife and slapped her when she would not let go of the chicken — three strokes!' He closed his book and shuffled back through the crowd. Bingo was waving the whip to the crowd, and then he whipped the poor guy, who fainted on the first stroke, the crowd cheered, and then the dancing started up, with the drums going and the occasional shot fired into the air, it was pandemonium. Murphy came over,

'And how are you, young man?' I raised my voice above the din,

'I need a word with you.' We retired to the beer hall, I ordered a beer, and Murphy rubbed his chest, 'Still got that cough.' I ordered a double whisky. Murphy's eyes lit up, 'God bless you, my son.' His hand was shaking as he put the glass to his mouth.

'Now, I must warn you that there is trouble up in the north, the rebels have captured a small town and some villages, they killed everybody in a missionary post, the Congolese troops fled at the first shots, and some of the troops did not even have rifles.' I shook my head and muttered. Murphy nodded, then took a long sip from his glass. He paused as if he had remembered something. 'Oh, and something else, some of the soldiers stationed here are from the same ethnic tribe as the rebels.'

I got Murphy another whisky and went back to my compound, checked my bag with the thirty thousand dollars, and planned my next trip to Antwerp.

Over Sunday breakfast, Archie and Pete complained that they had had enough of the boredom, steamy heat, and flies, and they had decided to leave for the UK next week. I was devastated, although it made me feel easier to bail out when the time came.

That night after everyone was asleep, I crept out, said. 'Hi' to the guards then muttered

'Can't sleep.' Got into my jeep and drove down into the jungle mud road, it was pitch black. With headlights on to see the road, I parked at the big tree. My torch lit the way along the overgrown path till I reached the tree, turning right two metres then started digging, in moments my pick hit the box, and I took out the remaining three bags, two full bags and one-half full. I put the bags into the jeep and covered them. so far, so good. I drove back to the barracks and put the bags into the box under my bed. Monday morning, I accompanied the Brits to the mine,

I wanted to check that all was well, I had already promoted two of the miners as foremen.

Once a month an armoured truck and two open-top trucks full of Congo soldiers would arrive at the mine to collect the stones that had been mined, the Belgian officer in charge had a key and the combination to a huge safe set into concrete in one of the concrete sheds.

They carried out leather bags full of stones, and then, just as quickly as they had arrived, they were gone, so somebody at the mine had to have the spare key and knew the combination.

Two white South African engineers lived in a jungle village. Could one of them be the key holder? I decided to meet them.

I walked into the mine with two Brits, the noise and dust were everywhere. A little way into the mine was lit up with a string of lamps hanging from the roof. A large wooden shed sat at the side of the tunnel. knocking hard above the noise, the door was opened by a white guy holding a gun. Lowering the gun he shook my hand,

'Hi, boss man what can I do for you?'

'I just came to introduce myself.' 'I said.

The two Brits lit up cigarettes and waited outside.

As I stepped into the shed, another guy was shaving at a sink wearing a vest, and a key hanging from his neck, he laid the razor down and shoved the key down his vest, then carried on shaving.

'You are lucky to catch us here, we are going to Brazzaville tomorrow for some R and R'. Waving to a chair, I sat and was served tepid coffee. There was a knock on the door and a miner covered in dust, handed a stone over to the South African, he was given a pack of cigarettes and a can of beer, and then the door was shut. I noticed one of the guys putting the stone into a cupboard.

Although we chatted about everything under the sun, diamonds were never mentioned. Saying I have things to do, we shook hands as I left, I had solved the puzzle of who oversaw the stones.

I walked out of the noise and dust into the sunshine, oppressive heat, and flies.

I informed the Belgian officer that I was going back to London for a few days to sort out family affairs. Panic showed on his face, as he said,

'Ok, but don't be too long, look what happened last time,...and bring me back some decent cigars.'

Sitting on my metal bed, the curtain was drawn open by a Congolese soldier, I recognised him as an adjutant from the Belgium officer's close circle. He saluted me and said in broken English that his boss needed to speak with me—Now.

I followed him out to the compound that held his tiny office. The soldier knocked once, opened the door, stepped to the side, and waved me in. The officer sat at a metal desk covered in files and documents. Without looking up, he waved for me to sit.

There was silence as he studied something lying in front of him. He threw the document to one side, looked up and leaned across the desk. He stared at me for a full five seconds, then shook his head, and said,

'Trouble my friend, trouble. I've had a call from the defence minister to send you and your men to a village on the edge of Ango, A day's drive from here. The soldiers guarding the diamond mine have not been paid for a month, and have gone on a rampage, killing the general and his commander, who belonged to a different tribal group. Both of them were related to the President.

The minister sent a colonel with a package of money and promises, hoping to placate the soldiers. In a drunken rage, the leaders of the mob took the money and shot dead the colonel and his driver.' He shook his head, 'It's corruption again. Some minister in charge of finance have had their hands in the till and blamed a computer mistake or a junior for a calculation error.

The finance minister is putting relatives or bosom buddies into positions in the government. They are landowners or tribe elders who support him, so to strengthen him, they become ministers in charge of departments with no experience. They quickly start to skim money off the budgets and demand money for various permits or licences. The government minister who gave them the job expects a cut. The corruption got so bad that foreign investors were pulling out. The president had to clamp down. Three ministers were shot, five fled to France and others got thrown into jail.' He knew the army generals were corrupt, but most of them were relatives or people from the same tribe.' He smirked. The Mafia looked like Boy Scouts compared to some of these guys.'

He took a cigar from a bamboo cigar box, there was a pause as it took several attempts to produce a glow. He turned with a look of satisfaction, then said,

'I have to instruct you to take your men and put down the rebellion before it spreads.' He slowly placed the smoking cigar into a large marble ashtray, then leaned across, 'They are mostly boy soldiers that were given rifles and uniforms, but there are two sergeants from the regular army I don't know if they are leading the rebellion or being held hostage' He sat back into his chair, 'Most of them have returned to their villages with whatever they looted from the village they were supposed to protect. I know that a group of them are still

in the village. He lowered his voice,

'Find the ringleaders and kill them, orders from the chief of the army...Mobutu.'

He picked up the cigar and said, 'No trials, no long drawn out who did what. News travels fast, and a quick put-down will send the message to other tribesmen in the army thinking of revolting, who will remember what happened to the last revolt. So, make it brutal and final.' If it reaches the European press, they will believe it was tribal warfare. The overseas news stations are only interested in bodies lying on the ground and tribesmen saying to the cameras how another tribe had attacked them.

Chapter 13

I took Archie and Pete with seven other guys. All European special forces soldiers. All trained in jungle warfare tactics. Ten of us got on a bus, armed to the teeth. The ancient army bus took us on a six-hour journey to the village on the outskirts of Agno. A small town surrounded by several villages. Darkness had fallen as we drove through the jungle along the cinder road and pulled into the quiet square of the village, surrounded by tin shanty huts. The plan had been to stop a hundred yards from the village, and approach on foot, identifying traps and waiting for shooters. Basic tactics. There had been a misunderstanding with the driver on the approach. However, the village was quiet until barking dogs announced our arrival.

An old man holding a flickering oil lamp with a dozen dogs running around his legs shuffled from a hut to the bus. He looked in amazement at European soldiers holding rifles at the ready climbed off the bus. A shot from the edge of the jungle made everyone hit the ground. The old man crouched and shuffled away, followed by the dogs.

The bullet shattered a bus window. Although the guys on the bus were bleary-eyed when they stepped off the bus. The shot got their attention. The returning fire was immediate and silenced the shooter. The Brits were lying on the ground, weapons ready to fire at the next flash from the shooter.—Basic practice. I hoped that the shooter was a drunk soldier taking a pot shot in our direction with a standard-issue rifle.

My worst fear was that it was a trained sniper with a night scope. Another shot shattered another window. I let out a breath, my first assumption was right. The Brits sent a volley of bullets at the muzzle flash in the trees.

Lights were appearing from some of the huts, and shadowy figures were staggering out partly dressed, holding weapons. Three figures dropped their rifles and ran into the jungle.

A Voice shouted a muffled order in French, then other figures started firing at the bus. In the darkness, it was the only thing visible. The firing took out the remaining windows, but it also gave the Brits. their targets. Most of the rebels were standing at the doors with a light behind them, making perfect targets. The Brits kept up steady firing for ten seconds. When they stopped an eerie silence fell over the village. Even the monkeys stopped screaming as if they knew the shooting was over. Bodies were lying by the doors. Shafts of light fell over dead men holding rifles. The Brits slowly stood and walked to the bodies. Every few seconds a shot would finish off a wounded man. I told myself that if I stopped my men finishing off the wounded, what could I do with them?

If I left them to be cared by the villagers I knew they would be slaughtered in revenge for their past actions, plus they were from a different ethnic tribe which would seal their fate.

An elderly woman ran out of the darkness and spoke to me in French, then broken English. She pointed to a hut at the end of the village, and mouthed,

'Daughter, my daughter, there.' She pointed again,

then threw her arms around her chest and gave the image of a struggle.

I took a New Zealand guy called Benny with me and we crept along the row of huts to the end. A light shone from under the door. As Benny stepped back and covered me, I slowly turned the handle, inching the door open and glanced inside. The room was bathed in light from two oil lamps that stank. Two rebel soldiers lay sleeping. One lay on a crude straw bed holding a Glock-19 pistol on his chest, the other lay on his side on the floor, clutching an empty beer can and snoring, a rifle lay at his side. *How did the shooting not wake them?* A girl was crouched in a corner and stared as I crept in. As I glanced at her bruised face and the dried blood under her nose, the guy with the pistol leapt to his feet and pointed the pistol at my head. A shot rang out and he slumped down with a tiny hole in his forehead. Benny stood in the doorway and smiled, and then the other rebel turned around and reached for his rifle, still holding the beer can in his other hand. Benny and I fired together. The rebel had drunk his last can of beer. The girl ran crying into her mother's arms. The remaining rebels had fled into the jungle. An elder pointed to a ditch where we found the bodies of the two Congolese army sergeants.

Dawn was rising above the trees as the Brits were given food and beer from the grateful villagers. I asked the radio guy to check with the Brits back at the diamond mine, and all seemed well, except for a punch-up in the bar between soldiers from different tribes. We decided to leave after a couple of locals said there was no sign of soldiers in the jungle. The old driver had cleared out the glass and was muttering about compensation. One side of the bus was peppered with bullet holes. Everyone got on the bus as villagers came over and handed us clay jugs of foul-tasting beer.

With a roar from the engine and clouds of diesel smoke choking the onlookers, we left, followed by children and barking dogs. Most of the guys slept for six hours to Mbuji-Mayi, despite the pot-holes and an engine that sounded as if it hadn't an exhaust. We arrived in the darkness, unloaded our weapons and kit, then everyone headed for the barracks that held the bar. This was standard procedure after returning from a mission. The old guy on the piano was belting out his version of the Marseillaise, with a crowd of drunk Congolese soldiers providing the chorus, and four Brits linked arms and sang, 'Rule Britannia.' Each group sings louder

The Brits. were sometimes referred to as the 'Fire brigade' unit on account of having been sent by the Congolese Army to trouble spots in the Congo to quell trouble between different tribes, but more and more with the various warlords. The Congolese Army was made up of different tribal groups. So, unless they were sent to 'sort out' a non-ethnic tribe, it would usually end in a shoot-out.

One mission was to a village on the Rwanda border.

A warlord had been killed by a group of his soldiers who hadn't been paid for months. The boy soldiers had no loyalty to any particular tribe only to those that paid the most. They were known to change sides in the middle of a firefight. Then joined up with another mercenary group, led by an ex-foreign legionnaire called 'Chapeau Blank' on account of his white Stetson cowboy hat. He and his men were chased over the border from Rwanda into the Congo and they were heading for this village. The reason we were sent there was because it was the village that had relatives of a Congolese General.

After a day's journey in two yellow American ex-school buses, we arrived at the edge of the village to learn that an advanced group of boy soldiers had already arrived and killed the chief and three elders when they refused to give them money. We stepped off the buses to see three mutilated bodies lying in the square. Two had been beheaded. Kids and dogs walked around them as if it were a normal event. Three kids as young as twelve were leaning against a fence, carrying AK-47 assault rifles over their shoulders and cartridge belts around their necks. Chatting to each other, smoking marijuana, and drinking beer. Looking at us getting off the buses, stared for a moment then carried on chatting. They assumed we were more soldiers from the same group. I ordered everybody from the buses to form a line with weapons held at the ready. One of our Congolese escorts walked in front and pulled a rifle from the nearest rebel, making him spill his beer. Everything changed in a second, the other two dropped the beer cans and swung their rifles off their shoulders as I shouted, 'Fire' *It was them or us?*

The blast of gunfire sent the three kids to the ground.

Kids, dogs, and villagers scattered to the safety of the jungle and as other boy soldiers appeared out of the huts, firing at them made most run into the jungle. The ones that stopped to fire back were easily cut down. Three minutes later it was all over. We counted seven dead kids and three wounded, who were brutally killed by some of the villagers with machetes who took revenge for their dead chief.

We stayed in the village until we learned that the main force had taken a wide berth of the village when learning that a British mercenary group was ready to protect the villagers.

Chapter 14

On one of my daily trips to Franke's office in the compound. After solving some minor problems, I got up to leave as he opened a draw in his desk and said,

,'Hold on, I have a packet for you it arrived this morning.'

Pulling out an A4 size brown envelope he handed it to me, 'Good news I hope,' and laughed.

Sitting back in the chair, I tore it open, inside was a dog tag the kind soldiers wear around their necks. Nothing unusual about that except the tag belonged to Archie my lifelong friend. The last time I saw him was only two days ago at the mine, and nothing unusual about that, he would sometimes go on a bender and drop off the world for a couple of days, but I've never known him to lose his dog tag. He once told me that he never took it off, not for a shower, not for a woman, not ever. I upended the envelope over the desk and tapped it, it only held the dog tag. No stamp only my handwritten name. Asking Franke how he got it, he shrugged his shoulders and said,

'Someone must have pushed it under my door before I arrived this morning. The guard is still on duty he might have seen someone, but they would have to get past him to get to my office.

Walking out to the gate, the Congolese soldier was leaning against the gate lighting a cigarette.

Waiting for him to take a lung full of smoke, I asked if he'd seen anyone. He blew smoke then coughed,

'Sure, a little guy I haven't seen before said he had a letter for Franke, I took it from him, and when he had gone, I went to Franke's office and shoved it under the door. So, what's the problem, not a bomb I hope!'

He laughed, then took a drag and coughed. I went back to my barracks and saw Pete as he came back from the shower, and asked when last he saw Archie.

He told me that the last time he saw Archie, he was deep in conversation with a middle-aged French woman in the bar, and he told me she had invited him back to her Hotel for a drink. Pete winked and said,

'I guess Archie knew what she meant.'

I overheard her say she was staying at the Hotel Bassora just a few miles outside town.

I took a jeep and drove the few miles to the carpark of the Hotel. The receptionist was a pretty girl with a huge Afro. Giving me a wide smile showing metal braces, she said,

'And how can I help, sir.'

I explained that I was looking for a friend who may be staying with a lady at this Hotel. The girl gave a sly grin and then stared at the computer, and said,

'And her name?'

'Sorry, I didn't get her name, only that she was French—and middle-aged.'

Staring at the computer, she tapped on the screen,

'Three women are staying at the Hotel this week,

Madam Leon is an elderly woman in a wheelchair, and Mrs Barlow is an American woman with a Congolese husband' She paused, and stared at the screen again,

'And a Madam Francine du belay. But she left last night, her husband had to be helped into her car. and he looked to be unconscious,

'Describe him.' She put a finger to her chin, and said,

'He was a European in his thirties wearing an army uniform, I thought that was a little strange, but I was told not to ask questions.'

'Do you know where they went?' I asked.

She shook her head making the Afro wobble. I put a fifty-dollar note on the desk and left for Raj and the bar, the guy who knew everybody and everything that was happening. Putting a beer in front of me, he said,

'Yeah, Archie was talking to Francine and left with her, why do you ask?' 'Because Archie has disappeared. I traced him to the

Bassora Hotel and the receptionist told me that he was unconscious when they left in a car.'

Raj leaned over the bar, then looked around,

'Francine du Belay' he whispered, 'Is a 'friend' of Bingo. He helped her get a permit to live in the Congo.' He paused as two soldiers walked in.

'She and her husband ran a gang that kidnapped tourists and held them for ransom before the Ugandan police arrested them. Her husband got ten years, but most of her gang and she escaped to the Congo. It looks like she is back to her old ways. If I was you, I'd pay any ransom she asks for. In Uganda they shot a tourist who tried to escape after his wife refused to pay, the guy they shot was a retired American diplomat so the police had to track the gang down and arrest them to avoid bad publicity.'

I had heard of gangs raiding villages and kidnapping women and village chiefs for ransom, but I thought that only happened deep in the jungle.

Walking to my barracks, my phone buzzed,

A woman spoke English with a strong French accent

'If you want your friend returned in one piece, you will leave a packet containing ten thousand American dollars with your friend Raj, with orders to hand it to a man who tells him he is 'Le collecteur' if the money isn't there by tomorrow evening, we will tell you where you can find his body, comprendre! The phone clicked off. Raj said she was a friend of Bingo. Strolling to his compound and passing a guard sitting on a battered armchair by the door. Bingo was at his desk watching a football game on a TV hanging from the wall. Without looking to see who came in, he waved to a chair. On the screen, a player had missed a penalty. Bingo groaned and turned to face me,

'Hello my friend,—what do you want?'

'Your friend, Francine du Belay has made a mistake in kidnapping one of my men for ransom, she doesn't realize that if he isn't released unharmed, we will hunt her and her gang down and kill them all!

Bingo turned to look at the TV, and apart from the noise of the football match no one spoke for a minute. Bingo wheeled around and slapped his desk,

'I don't know any Francine du Belay but I'll see what I can find out, now if you don't mind, I am trying to watch this match.' He glanced at the TV and said,

'And close the door behind you.'

As I left closing the door, I put my ear to the wood and heard a phone being lifted from its cradle and Bingo's muffled voice talking to someone in French.

Early the next morning Archie stepped from a taxi and was surrounded by three guys all speaking at once, where did they hold you? Did they threaten to kill you? He told them he was drugged and blindfolded most of the time, and then all of a sudden, he was driven into town and thrown into a taxi.

The taxi driver cut his bonds off, and removing the blindfold drove him to the barracks.

Chapter 15

A month later I was summoned to a meeting in Franke's office. Two Belgian officers and a Congolese major were sitting at his desk. I was waved to sit and I knew what was coming!

From time to time, we were seconded to other ex-Belgium colonies to act as security for visiting Western diplomats or leaders from other African states, some democratic others by army generals that had grabbed power and ruled by banning or jailing any other political that had not fled the country. On one such mission seven of us were flown to a military base in Rwanda then helicoptered to Lake Kivu and put up in a luxury hotel overlooking the beach.

The guy we were guarding was a Rwandan General, Francois Nkosi a cousin of the President who was 'elected' after an army coup. The entire top floor was taken over by Nkosi and his three wives. The lower floors were for the Brits. and his Rwandan bodyguards.

I was called to his room for a meeting the day we arrived. Two armed Rwandan soldiers escorted me to the General's room door, patted me down and took my pistol.

Entering the huge lounge, a tall middle-aged woman dressed in Western clothes waved me to sit at the dining table then spoke in French into a shoulder mike. Moments later a bedroom door opened and an older tall grey-haired guy dressed in army uniform walked in, shook my hand and with a broad grin said in perfect English, 'I am General Francois Nkosi, head of Rwandan security services'

Without breaking his stare, he put his hand in the air, snapped his fingers, and shouted something in French. Another door opened and two younger women in western dress walked in, each carrying a large gym bag, placed them on the table and left. Francois grinned as he patted the bags and said,

'Half a million American dollars, a gift from me my friend, I trust this will ensure your loyalty?' He stared at me then dropped his voice, 'There's no need to tell your men of this gift.' Leaning over I tapped his arm,

'That's not how it works, if I kept all the money, I would lose the respect of my men and that's not worth a half-million dollars! He leaned back looking surprised, then stood and said,

'As you wish.'

We took shifts guarding his room door. Two guys sitting on chairs, with AK 47s. across their laps. Another two were in the hotel lobby checking on people entering the lift or stairs, the rest sleeping in their room or at the bar playing cards with the Rwandan soldiers whom we had replaced. The scene looked like a wild-west saloon with two British merceries, rifles propped against chairs and bar girls standing behind them.

Escorting General Nkosi and his entourage to various townships and mining complexes where he would give the same speeches and promises of better things from the government.

We would always return to the hotel by Lake Kivu.

One morning I was awakened by shouting and the sound of people running in the lobby. One of the Brits. Came in and said that there had been a coup in the capitol and an army General had taken over. I dressed and rushed to the General's room. He was sitting at the table on the phone while his wives were rushing around packing bags. Francois grabbed my hand his voice was shaking as he said that he wanted my soldiers to take him and his wives to a waiting jet at a nearby strip. He whispered that he didn't trust his bodyguards. We gathered outside with suitcases filled with money and boarded three army trucks.

He shouted to his Rwandan bodyguards that he would return the trucks for them to join him. Some smiled, they had heard of the coup and they knew that General Nkosi was fleeing.

Twenty bumpy minutes later we drove onto the tarmac where a small Lear jet was waiting. Nkosi, his wives and bags of American dollars were shoved on board. Few words were spoken before the door closed and they blasted off. The jet was a spot in the sky when wailing police cars and three jeeps of Rwandan soldiers arrived as the jet disappeared into the clouds. An army major stepped forward waving a document and said,

'You are all under arrest for assisting the escape of a wanted man.' I smiled as he pulled out his revolver. As if I had given an order, the seven Brits. lifted their rifles and clicked off the safety. The major looked at the police chief then slowly holstered his revolver, walked backwards to his jeep, and drove away in a cloud of dust followed by the police car. I let out a long breath as the vehicles disappeared in a cloud of dust.

I knew it was time to get out while we could before that Major returned with more troops. We would all be killed in a firefight or surrender and be held for ransom in some stinking prison for months. The distance from Lake Kivu in Rwanda to the Congo border was a day's journey in an army truck, then another day to Mbuji-Mayi, and safety.

We took two of the best trucks we could find and set off an hour later. A long bumpy ride later we were almost empty when we pulled into a gas station ten miles from the Congo border to fill up and buy food and water from the many roadside vendors. The kid who filled the tanks was a Tutsi, a tribe that had been massacred in the past and hated the ruling Hutus. Smiling he told me in broken English that trucks of Hutu soldiers were an hour behind us and the radio told him that we had stolen half a million dollars from a hotel and if the pursuing soldiers caught us, they could keep half the money and return the other half to the general now in charge. Quickly loading as much food and water as we could, we roared off.

As we approached the Congo border post, we voted to shoot our way through if they tried to detain us. The border guards will have heard on their radio that we were carrying money. They may take the money and hand us over to the pursuing soldiers because if we were captured by the Rwanda soldiers, they would march us to the nearest forest and shoot us all. Driving up to the barrier, the Brits were ready for a shootout. I was shocked to see the barrier lifted and Congolese guards waving us through.

Pulling into a layby to stretch our legs and eat and let the trucks cool down, I shared out the half million dollars before we arrived at a Congolese army base a mile over the border.

After convincing the officer in charge that we were employed by the Congolese government, and after a couple of calls to Franke at Mbuji-Mayi, we were helicoptered to another army airstrip. After a meal and a few beers in the canteen, we boarded a World War Two twin prop-Dakota. There were no seats, so we sat on the floor drinking beer and celebrating our good fortune *and the money*

It was dark when some hours later we landed at a single airstrip and a waiting helicopter that flew us 'home' to Mbuji-Mayi.

We were still on a high when we marched in the darkness to the beer hall and a grinning Raj. Sitting with the guys we toasted each and I remembered Archie's words before we left the Glasgow hotel, 'Why are they paying this money when they can get the local cops to do it?'

Late the next morning I met with Franke at his compound and gave him our report, (Forgetting the money.) As we were talking about the incidents, his door opened, and a Congolese guy in a major's uniform holding a briefcase stepped in. Franke introduced him and he sat next to me and said in broken English,

'I am in charge, of security at an open-cast gold mine near the gold mine of Kibali in Haut-Uele province in North-East Congo. I have lost control of my soldiers, some of them have sold their weapons and joined the gold diggers who are illegally selling the gold to the Arab traders. The miners get ten per cent of the value of the gold they give to the government officials, the Arabs give them fifty per cent. When I sent my soldiers to the gold fields to arrest the deserters, they said they were threatened with a shoot-out, but the truth was the deserters and my soldiers belonged to the same tribe, and I heard that the Arabs gave them money. Unfortunately, my soldiers haven't been paid their full wages for two months and if they aren't paid this month, some of them will desert and go to work in the gold fields.' I glanced at Franke. We both knew it was another case of corruption. Somewhere, between the money being sent from army headquarters and the major,

a government official was taking a cut from the money. The major raised his voice, 'I need you and your men to arrest the deserters, chase off the Arabs and protect the officials who control the gold fields. We will pay you and your men in cash double what you're getting here. I have spoken with the interior minister and he agrees. He opened his briefcase to show me American dollars neatly packed to the top. Then said,

'This is for you when you and your men arrive in Kibali.' Then he shut the case and took it off the desk. I wondered if that money was from the soldier's wages! I explained to the major that the first week he missed paying my men, we would return to Mbuji-Mayi

'But of course, I am a man of my word.' He said.
I would have refused the offer it sounded too much like trouble but Franke told me the order wasn't a request, but an order from the top!

Chapter 16

The Congolese army was given the job of guarding the mine. As all the Brits. were told the orders and packed their stuff. Two refused and said they were returning to the UK. This wasn't the British army, we were mercenaries! Paid for their services, I couldn't force them to obey an order or court martial them. I felt more confident when Archie and Peter said they'd join me.

So, early one morning we set off to the airport in an army truck with eight grumbling soldiers, four crates of beer and all the equipment we could carry. We boarded an old American transporter with the seats taken out. As the guys sat with their backs to the plane's fuselage and passed around the beer, I went to speak to the pilot. I was a little surprised to see three Congolese girls in army uniforms, one sitting at the controls, another was the co-pilot and the third was sitting at the radio desk. The 'lady' pilot looked to be in her teens. She spoke to the other two in French, then turned to me, smiled, and holding out her hand, said in perfect English,

'My name is Naomi.' The other two giggled when she asked, 'Are there spare three beers back there?'

Telling her that I would get them a beer when we were airborne, Naomi smiled again, showing gleaming white teeth, she turned around and they all put on headphones. I joined the guys. Some were asleep, some were writing letters and others drinking beer and talking.

The plane bumped along the tarmac and it seemed like a long time before we lifted into the sky. I have flown many, many, times in prop-shaft planes and knew the sounds the engines made. After an hour the engine noise sounded different, a subtle change that no one seemed to notice. Grabbing three beers I made my way to the Cockpit. Naomi was staring at the control panel with the radio girl peering over her shoulder. I could tell something was wrong. Leaning over her other shoulder I stared at the dials. One of the engines wasn't firing on all cylinders. Naomi had increased the acceleration on the other engine to compensate. There was a small bang that came from the engine. We all looked out the window to see a thin thread of black smoke coming from the engine. Naomi's face was tense as she pulled a lever to shut down the engine. The plane seemed to slow down and slowly lose height. The co-pilot was franticly pumping a lever and staring across at the smoke billowing from the engine. Gradually the smoke faded to nothing, and then all the girls nervously smiled. Naomi turned and said,

'The engine has been extinguished, but we have used all the foam, if the engine ignites again, we have nothing left to put it out!' As I left the cockpit the girls were opening the beer bottles. The landing was as bumpy as the take-off. We had landed at a small military airport with one tarmac and concrete airstrip, a hanger was next to a single-storied concrete building with a corrugated tin roof that was a bar and customs post together. Fifty yards away a three-storied block built hotel was surrounded by jungle. Leaving everything piled outside.The guys headed into the bar.

A Congolese soldier waved me into the customs office at the end of the bar. Sitting opposite him at a metal desk, I watched as he thumbed through a pile of papers and handed some to me. they were all in French. I tried the only French I knew,

'Parley vous Anglaise?'

Looking puzzled he smiled and held his hand up as he left the table and strode into the bar. Moments later he walked in with Naomi who grabbed a chair. Sitting next to me she looked at the papers and said,

'These are telling you where to go and who to speak to, that is all, the rest is rubbish unless you are Congolese.

Taking her arm, we walked into the crowded bar.

'I guess I owe you a drink.' Smiling, she nodded to the young barman and said,

'I'll have my usual and this guy will have a beer.'

Holding a hand up, and looking at Naomi,

'This guy is called George, I said, and George would like a whisky—please.'

Naomi said something in French and they both laughed.

Finding a table, she told me that she had never been so frightened when the engine failed. She leaned over the table and whispered that her co-pilot had wet herself!

Then sat back and let out a loud laugh.

Naomi told me that her father was French and her mother was Congolese. He had returned to Paris when they divorced. Her mother had remarried and moved to Uganda when Naomi joined the military. Glanced at her watch, she drained her glass, and said,

'You and your soldiers are staying at the airport hotel tonight, then in the morning the transport will take you to the army barracks near the gold fields.

I am going to my room at the hotel if you come with me, I'll show you your room, it's always the same one that they give to officers or important visitors.'

Taking my arm, we walked in the falling darkness to the hotel. No words were spoken as we stared at the elevator's shiny doors opening on the top floor. Naomi shook my hand, then pointing to a door said,

'That's your room,' she paused, 'I am two doors down.'

And walked away. The room was basic. A worn carpet and army metal bed. the Congolese flag was hanging from the white painted bare wall above a chest of drawers. I stripped and stepped into a shower. Turning the handle to hot, a spray of Luke-warm water was enough to wipe the sweat and stress away. Wrapping a bath towel around me, I peered into a deserted lobby and then crept to Naomi's room. Knocking once and trying the handle the door opened and I stepped in. Naomi came out of the bathroom with a towel wrapped around her and her hair covered in a towel turban. Grinning she said,

'And who said that you were invited, young man!'

Wrapping my arms around her, I kissed her, she paused and moved away, then pushed into me and kissed me hard. Her towel dropped to the floor.

I awoke to the sound of a bugle and got out of bed. Naomi was asleep with her thumb in her mouth like a baby.

The guys had put their equipment onto a waiting army bus then went to the bar that had long tables for breakfast and coffee. When I joined them, I asked the cook for two soft-boiled eggs on brown toast and a mug of coffee, ten minutes later he put a tin plate in front of me with beans and burnt toast. When I complained he shrugged his shoulders, said something in French and walked away.

The bus journey was a mixture of smooth wide tarmac road with French speeding signs that ended abruptly, as if they had run out of tarmac! Then onto a narrow earth-packed 'road' with potholes every few metres. On both sides of the 'road' natives wearing loin cloths and shorts were digging, and others were working sifting the earth in long wire boxes with running water. Most of them were covered in dark mud. There seemed to be hundreds of holes as far as the eye could see. We drove another mile and the 'road' continued into the distance. We stopped at a line of blue tents on either side of the 'road' They looked like surplus UN emergency refugee tents. Each one held two army field beds a cupboard and wash bowls. At the end of the row was a block-built shower unit and a toilet that we could smell as we stepped off the bus. There were surprisingly few grumbles, most of the guys had spent months living in less 'luxurious' accommodations when they were on manoeuvres or missions, so this didn't seem too bad for a short time. There was a wooden shed the size of a single garage at the beginning of the tents this was the 'office' of a Congolese major who came daily, he lived in the airport hotel. As the guys settled in, I walked to the office.' An American SUV was parked at the side and two Congolese soldiers were guarding the door. As I came to the door they stepped aside and I walked in.

A bare bulb hung from the ceiling giving the room a cold eerie feel. The major looked up and nodding, waved me to sit at the desk. I noticed a black briefcase at his feet.

'I see you have finally arrived.' The major pulled out a pack of American cigarettes and lit one, blowing smoke to the roof,

'But only eight men?' he said. 'You won't restore order with only eight men! I expected at least twenty soldiers.'

Pushing his chair back, he stood, turned his back, and said,

'The deal is off, I will hold the money till I see how your men perform, now go! I stepped over to him, grabbed his shirt and going nose to nose, I shouted,

'You knew exactly how many men were arriving, this is your corrupt way to get out of paying me. Now either pay me now, or me and my men are gone, orders or no orders!' The cigarette dropped from his hand,

'You can't leave—you've been ordered,' he said.

'I'll take over the control of your men.'

Letting go of his shirt, I stepped back and laughed,

'Do you think my soldiers are going to listen to you, even your men ignored your commands?'

Picking up the briefcase I opened the door, and said,

'We'll be ready to go to the gold fields tomorrow, meet me here at nine hundred hours and show us the problem.' He nodded a yes and straightened his collar.

Chapter 17

The heat was stifling as we boarded the battered army bus and followed the SUV with the major and his driver.

Twenty minutes later we arrived at a group of miners covered in mud and digging into the side of a low hill. As we walked towards them, three dropped their shovels and ran. The major turned to me and shouted,

'Shoot them, they are army deserters!'

Some of the Brits. lifted their rifles, then looked at me.

I shook my head and they lowered their weapons.

The miners, standing with their hands in the air, said something in French to the major. Then one opened a tin box lying beside some metal tools, pulled out a handful of Congolese dollars, handing them to the major.

They lowered their hands as the major nodded and put the money into his pocket. The major led us across piles of earth to another area where over ten men were sifting through stones and mud on a 'table' with water running through the stones like a stream. A young native in mud-covered shorts and long scars on his chest stepped towards the major and waving his arms, shouted in French. The major turned to me and said,

'Arrest that man—now!'

The natives at the 'table' stopped work and stared at us.

'What the hell is happening here' I shouted at the major,

'I am not going to arrest—or shoot anyone, until I know why you are demanding money!

As the major shouted, spittle flew from his mouth.

'These gold fields belong to the Congolese government and these miners have a fee to pay to dig for gold, and any gold they mine must be sold to the government officials at the going rate that is set by the interior ministry. You and your men are here to enforce the law.'

'What about the money that guy gave you? I said,

'I will hand that to the officials when they arrive.'He said.

Some of the Brits. laughed as others grinned. The major scowled and walked away, saying that he would put in a report to headquarters on my refusal to obey his orders.

The major had disappeared as we stood around the natives, some of my guys offered them cigarettes which were taken with wide smiles. One of the younger miners spoke English. He jumped out of the hole that was half-filled with water and got his cigarette lit, taking a draw, he said.

'We have to pay to work the gold fields, then get cheated when we sell the gold to the Army.'

We get ten per cent of the value of the gold from the government, but if we sell to the Arabs, they give us fifty per cent. The soldiers that were guarding the fields for the government hadn't been paid for a month so some went back to their villages, some joined a rebel army and some joined the miners. He has only twenty soldiers left, they are the ones he has paid and they won't come to the goldfields. The miners pay a gang of ex-soldiers to protect them, the last time the major came with his soldiers there was a shoot-out and four of the Congolese soldiers were killed and the rest ran away, so the ones that were left wouldn't come back to the fields, that's why you're here.'

We marched back to the bus and saw that the SUV had gone. Back at camp, I decided to find out the thoughts of the men, so over a beer, all of them agreed with me that the major was corrupt, and if we were to follow his orders there would be killings.

They voted to leave and return to Mbaji-Mayi I knew that if the major suspected we were leaving, he would make sure we couldn't find the bus and have the plane parked at another airport.

The next morning, we waited till the SUV arrived at the 'office' Then four of us charged in grabbed the major and his driver and tied them to the chairs while one man cut the phone wires and dismantled the radio. Eight men with rifles, an ammunition box and kit bags, crammed into a six-seater SUV and drove off past the gold fields, past the farms and into the airport.

The men unloaded their equipment and carried it to the bar/customs post, while I found the Dakota parked on the tarmac being refuelled by a six-wheeled tanker by two soldiers. Standing at the back of the tanker I waited till they had unhitched the hose and climbed into the truck, then stood at the door and asked the driver if he knew where the pilot was. He leaned out of the window shaking his head as if he didn't understand me, and drove off in a cloud of diesel smoke.

Walking into the bar, the radio was belting out French jazz music and the guys were standing at the bar. Naomi and the two girls were sitting at a table chatting to six Congolese soldiers at the next table. When she saw me, her face broke into a wide smile as she waved me over and pulled a chair from a table. Saying hello to the girls I kissed Naomi's cheek. Holding her hand in the air, she shouted to the barman for two double whiskies. She smiled as we touched glasses, took a sip then with a puzzled look, said,

'Why are your men here with their equipment?'

'We've been called back to Mbaji-Mayi, I said, 'You have to fly us there today!' I put the glass to my mouth and watched her pull out a notebook from her top pocket. Thumbing the pages, she looked up and said,

'Are you sure? All I've been given for today is to deliver two crates to Kahanga airport, leaving in two hours.'

'But Kahanga is only a hundred miles away, from Mbaji-Mayi and like I said, this is an emergency, the orders will probably come through to you soon, but we need to leave now!' Draining her glass, she flipped through her notebook again, said something in French to the two girls, then told me I would have to sign an order saying it was an emergency. Naomi and the two girls left the bar and headed for the plane as I shouted to the guys that we were leaving now!

We were all aboard and taxiing to the start on the tarmac when a crackling erupted from the radio. She held her hands to her earphones. I stood by Naomi's as she looked up and said,

'The flight controller thinks we are leaving early for Kahanga, what shall I tell him?' I was beginning to panic.

'I haven't time to explain my orders from Mbaji-Mayi, 'Just tell him you're leaving early for Kahanga.'

'Speaking for one minute, she pushed on the throttles making the plane shudder and move. Gaining speed and shaking violently I let out a long breath as we lifted into the sky. It was late evening when we touched down at a single concrete strip and as we came to a halt, I looked out a window to see a huge sign that said,

'Welcome to Kahanga airport' I walked into the cockpit as Naomi was taking off her headphones. I blurted out,

'Naomi, this isn't Mbuji-Mayi!' Looked at her co-pilot,

'Sorry George, but I'd be in trouble if I disobeyed orders,' she held up a hand, 'And as you said, it's only a hundred miles to Mbuji-Mayi. The cargo doors opened and a forklift truck pulled out a wooden crate.

Everyone trudged to the tiny airport bar, while I went in search of transport. At the back of the hangers, a space as big as a football field had high-wire fencing with French signs that said, 'No Entry' in English and French, held a dozen vehicles,' open top trucks, two buses and an American jeep. A small hut at the end of the compound had a light shining from a window.

The double gates were unlocked, so I pushed them open wide enough for a truck or a bus to get out, then walked over a gravel 'field' to the shed. Knocking once, the door was opened by an old man in an army overcoat holding a tiny dog. He said something in French and paused for an answer. I lifted my arms making a driving action,

'Bus, Bus, I said. He turned and shuffled to a board on a wall covered in vehicle keys. Without speaking he handed me a set of bus keys, stepped back, and closed the door. I couldn't believe my luck that it was that easy.

Unlocking the door of the first bus and checking the fuel gauge, it was full.

A maintenance sheet with ticks on the various items was lying on the dashboard. Turning the key, I drove slowly out of the compound and parked behind the bar. It looked like the civilian population of Kahanga was in that bar along with Congolese soldiers and Belgium officers. The Brits. we're sitting together at a long table drinking beer and sandwiches. Lowering my Voice, I told them to finish their beer and make their way to the back of the bar and board the bus. Collecting their equipment, they left the bar in twos and threes to not attract attention. Making their way around the bar they climbed into the bus. Watching the last two leaving the bar I waited to see if anyone noticed their going, then followed them out to the bus. Driving on a wide tarmac highway it took two hours before the lights of Mbuji-Mayi came into view. Then another half-hour before I drove up the main street, past the stalls and single-storied shacks with smoke filling the sky, blocking the moon. Putting their equipment and bags into the concrete barracks that was 'home'

Then everyone as was the custom, headed for the bar. Raj had managed to install a large screen TV to show French and African football. The huge satellite dish was an ex-military spy dish, when I asked Raj where he got it from, he smiled and put a finger to his lips.

Chapter 18

Everything seemed to be back to normal at the mine. Franke never brought up the subject of our quick return.

Archie and Pete had told me several times that they had enough of the Congo, and now they had enough money to enjoy life in the UK. They were leaving.

Speaking with Archie and Pete over a beer, Archie said,

'Let's go back to London together.' I nodded,

'But first I would have to promote two other guys to replace the 'late' Rall and Pel.' Pete raised a hand;

I had already given two miners the job, temporarily.

'I know the guys you need.' Said, Pete. I met the two Brits that Pete had recommended in the beer hall, we all sat down at a table, and I explained that they would be in charge, of getting the guys to the mine and other duties, they were Stan, a huge guy who had been a medic in the army, and Alec, a short, bald dude with a bad attitude. Over a beer, Alec told me that his wife had road-tested some of his mates while he was on manoeuvrers and that he planned to find her and her boyfriend and kill them when he got back to the UK.

I decided this was not the guy for the job, so I picked another Brit that I had spoken to before, Denis, he seemed an easy-going guy, who'd been a sergeant.

Over the next few days, I gave Stan and Denis the AK47s from Pete and Archie and paperwork, keys etc. On the day we were packing to leave, Denis told me that there was gunfire coming from the jungle, and the guy were nervous, I was too busy to take it seriously and said,

'Look, Denis, if it happens again, tell the Congolese officer.' I had twenty thousand dollars and three bags of stones on my mind!

Archie, Pete, and I set off to Maya-Maya airport at Brazzaville, a long dusty drive, when we eventually arrived it was evening, and there was not a flight to London till the next afternoon, so we booked into the airport hotel. I showered and changed into my last clothing. Throwing my dust-covered clothes into the bin and emptying a bottle of cologne from the bathroom over myself, I smelt like a tart when I met them in the bar. It's a great feeling to sit down with comrades. When we got settled at a table I said,

'I have a little present for you guys,' I pulled out two thousand dollars from my 'man bag' 'Here is the bonus that I told you about,' Archie's eyes widened,

'Wow, let's get pissed.' Pete murmured,

'Thanks, George, I don't know where this money came from...but thanks anyway,' Archie raised his voice,

'George told you it was a bonus from Brazzaville.' Pete put his head to one side and smirked, I stared Pete in the face,

'Have you heard the saying, never look a gift horse in the mouth.'

We ordered beers; Archie went to the toilet and came back with two giggling girls. Archie waved to the barman,

'Cocktails for the girls.' They were also catching the London flight. Pete had his arm around one of the girls and was whispering in her ear. Archie was telling tales, and I heard him say, 'Well, I am a major really.'

'George, work your magic and get a girl,' one of the girls pointed and said,

'The girl sitting at the end of the bar told me she was going back to London to meet her ex-boyfriend,' She leaned over and smiled, 'When the cats are away, the mice will play.' She laughed, and said,

'Give it a go, she looks like she could use some company!' I picked up my glass of Johnnie Walker wandered over and sat on the next stool, feeling a little sheepish, because I felt that she had heard us talking.'

'Hi, my name is George, can I get you a drink?'

She was a smartly dressed girl, about thirty-five, with dark brown hair curling to her shoulders and well-kept nails, she turned to smile with perfect teeth. Her face broke into a broad smile,

'I thought you would never ask!' she said,

That broke the ice. We both laughed, she said, 'My name is Olive.'

She glanced at my glass and said,

'I'll have whatever you're having,' I thought... have I heard that before?

Over drinks, we discussed Middle East affairs, which was her subject at university. No—she can't be a ten. Brains, sexy and drinks Johnnie Walker.

We sat chatting at the bar and she gave me a lecture on Middle East affairs. She could see from the look on my face that it wasn't my favourite subject. She kissed my cheek, and said,

'Look, George, why don't we go up to your room and we can discuss something else,' I nodded,

'Olive...I thought you would never ask.' We both grinned.

I went to the bar and got a bottle of black-label Johnnie Walker and two glasses.

In my room, Olive kicked her shoes off while I poured the drinks when I turned round to hand her a drink, she was standing naked, her clothes on the floor, her mouth curled into a slow smile, flashing those white perfect teeth,

'I hope you're not embarrassed, but I find this more comfortable,'...I wasn't complaining. Stripping, I joined her in bed, and kissing her, Olive muttered,

'Wait, wait, safety first' and handed me a condom. The next morning, I awoke and went to the bathroom, Olive was sitting on the toilet reading a magazine,

'Hurry up Olive, I am bursting for a leak.'

She looked at me, smiled and remarked,

'I see you are not Jewish.'

When I returned to the bedroom she was dressed and said,

'I am going to my room to shower and change; shall we meet downstairs for breakfast?' I nodded,

120

'Yes, I would like that,' I showered and got changed, checked my bag, taking a couple of hundred dollars with me.

Downstairs I looked around a half-empty dining room, no Archie, no Pete, no girls. I sat at a table and ordered eggs Benedict, with toast and fresh orange juice. I was halfway through the eggs when Olive joined me. She looked beautiful, hair perfect, with minimal make-up, and wearing a business suit.

She kissed my cheek and sat down as the waitress came to the table. I asked,

'What would you like Olive?'

She glanced at my half-empty plate, before Olive could speak, I said to the waitress,... 'She will have what I am having,' we both laughed. As we chatted over coffee, I paused, 'Olive, I wonder if you could help me?

I have some merchandise to get past the customs.' She put her coffee down and her head dropped...

'Is it drugs? George, I thought this was too good to be true.'

'No Olive,' shaking my head, 'I would not touch drugs, it's a couple of thousand American dollars.' She smiled as she picked up her coffee,

'Where would I put the money? 'Grinning, I pointed to her skirt, and said,

'Down your pants!' she looked stunned,

'Have you seen the size of my underwear,' she laughed, 'My mother calls them string knickers,' I said,

'Look, we will go shopping for grannie pants, big enough to hold the money.'

Chapter 19

We caught a taxi into town to a shopping arcade, I gave Olive some money, and fifteen minutes later she appeared with a bag. We took a taxi back to the hotel and up to my room.
Olive sashayed out of the bathroom and with a broad grin lifted her skirt to show me the grannie pants, they went from her belly button down to above her knees. We both fell onto the bed laughing. Later we went looking for Pete and Archie. Downstairs we found the girls sitting at the bar. I asked.

'Where were Pete and Archie?

One of the girls said,

'After they left the bar Pete said he wanted to go to a club,' she glanced at her friend, 'But we didn't want to go, so the guys got a taxi and left,' she smiled, 'They were both drunk.'

'Shall I ring the cop shop and see if they are in there.' Olive said,

Finding the hotel phone booth, Olive spoke French on the phone...*Was there no end to this girl's talents?* After what seemed like a long conversation, she replaced the phone and said through a laughing face,

'They are in jail, and will be there until tomorrow, then face a judge.' I asked,

'What's the charge?' Olive smiled,

'Pissing on a police car '

I went to the receptionist and paid for hotel security to collect their belongings, including the cash, and hold them till they came back.

When it was time to get to the plane, Olive followed me to the room. I took twenty thousand dollars and helped Olive stuff the money into her granny pants, making it all smooth and with no bumps, she put on a flared skirt, then stepped back and posed.

'How do I look?' she asked.
I shook my head and grinned,

'My, my, Olive you have put on weight!'

I gathered her suitcases and my bag with the stones and set off to the airport. As we approached the customs desk I stiffened and held my breath—So much for my practising looking casual. I stared straight ahead as we strode through the 'nothing to declare channel'. Olive murmured,

'See, that was easy.'

Boarding the plane, I kept looking around, waiting for a tap on my shoulder and only relaxing when the doors were closed and the seatbelt sign came on.

After five minutes in the air, Olive stood up, whispering,

'I need to pee,' ten minutes later she was back. She patted her hip, 'That was a struggle with all that money in the granny pants.' Moments later a flight attendant came up to our seats, she spoke to Olive in French and handed her a few dollar bills. When she had gone, Olive grinned and remarked,

'They must have dropped out when I pulled my pants up.'

At Heathrow, we gingerly came to the customs desk. Olive gave the young customs officer, I know what you're thinking smile, and she was waved through.

'Anything to declare sir. The elderly officer looked old school. His voice rang in my ear, 'Open your bag, sir.' Breaking into a sweat as I pulled the zip open, the customs guy peered in,

'What's that in the bag, sir?'

'Stones!' I muttered.

'Show me one sir,' I took out one that still had mud clinging to it, he looked bemused,

'What is that?' I took a deep breath,

'I am a palaeontologist, and these are samples for my students to study.' He had a puzzled look as he put a chalk mark on the bag and waved me through. He had just mistaken million-dollar diamonds, for stones!

I met up with Olive, and she said,

'You are shaking, let's get a drink.'

Sitting at the airport bar, I handed Olive a shopping bag to take to the toilet and get out of the grannie pants and the money. and ordered drinks to calm my nerves.

Olive returned twenty minutes later with the money in the bag, sat down and said,

'You trusted me, didn't you? 'I could have walked out of the airport with twenty-five thousand dollars to spend in the shops.' She put her arms around my neck and gave me a sloppy kiss and said, 'I love you.' Taking a sip of her drink, she announced,

'I must go round to see my mother in London. Shall I see you again?' I nodded and said,

'Olive, I have some business to do in Antwerp, why don't you come with me.' She put her head to one side,

'Will I have to wear the grannie pants?' I smiled and nodded,

'Probably,'

'Luckily, I kept them,' she said. We both laughed.

Once again, I booked into the airport hotel. I kissed Olive goodbye and we arranged to meet the next day at the hotel. I showered and changed then went down to a very glitzy bar.

Getting into small talk with a sales guy when I felt a tap on my shoulder, turning around, I froze... There was Rene, the young Belgian cop from Brazzaville. He shook my hand, and said,

'What are you doing in London, my friend?'

'Family matters!' I stuttered. 'And what are you doing in London, Rene?' He explained that since Mobutu took over the country, he wanted to modernise the security services and Rene was sent to London on a forensics course.

'So, you got the letter from the Brazzaville police with the results of the explosion?'

'Yes, yes,' I stammered, desperately trying to change the subject. 'Please, let me get you a drink,' Rene shook his head,

'No, I am with the group at the table,' he pointed over to a table with six middle-aged Congolese guys in sharp suits and Congolese leopard skin hats, who waved like robots.

When he went, I ordered a double whisky and downed it with a shaking hand. The sales guy looked concerned and asked,

'Everything ok? You have gone a little pale.' I tapped my chest,

'A little heart problem.' In the morning I went down to breakfast of two soft-boiled eggs and lots of coffee.

I wondered what had happened to Pete and Archie.

At eleven there was a knock on my room door and in sauntered my beautiful Olive in a smart grey dress and matching jacket. In high heels, she was as tall as me.

Going downstairs, we sat down for coffee and toast as I explained that I had uncut diamonds to take to a client in Antwerp, telling her it was another job for the granny pants,

'If I must,' she said with a grin.

'But my lovely, we are going into town to buy some clothes for our trip.'

She clapped her hands. 'Super!' I grabbed one of her hands and said,

'But first I want you to phone the Brazzaville police and find out what has happened to Pete and Archie?' We went downstairs and Olive spoke to the Brazzaville police, she put the phone down,

'They got three days in jail and a hundred francs fine, the policeman said on the phone, that it was only going to be a small fine until an English man called the judge a pratt. When the judge got the translation, he gave them three days in jail.' I slapped the table.

'Idiots! Why could they not keep their mouths shut,' then we both laughed.

Taking a taxi into town. Olive bought shoes, and more shoes, some underwear and perfume which cost more than one pair of shoes!! I got a suit and shoes a couple of expensive shirts, underpants and socks, and a huge, wheeled suitcase. The total bill was twelve hundred dollars, I was about to moan about the cost, then remembered the money I had hidden and thought, what was twelve hundred bucks!

Laden with boxes and bags we took a taxi back to the hotel. After a drink at the bar to calm down, it was time to make tracks to the airport. We had stuffed everything into the wheeled case.

Olive stuck the stones into the grannie pants, and I put half the money into my bag and the rest in my trousers.

My heart rate rose as we went through customs, But this time without a hitch. Boarded the plane and we were off to Antwerp. Sitting on the plane, Olive kept scratching between her legs. I grinned and said, 'Have you got the crabs dear?'

Giving me a stern look and then whispered,

'Certainly not! It's those stones in my pants!' She grinned, 'Same as ants in my pants, only bigger—and worth more.'

Landing at the airport, we took a taxi to the same small hotel near the diamond Centre. The young guy behind the desk recognized me as I said,

'Two nights please.'

Handing over our passports we went to the room.

Olive got out of the granny pants and put the stones into my small bag. We showered together and she gave me a private show of her new underwear. We dressed and walked to a restaurant nearby, ordering soup and fish with a huge bowl of ice cream. After a few beers, we staggered back to the hotel. flopped into bed, kissed goodnight, and slept like babies.

Chapter 20

In the morning we went down to breakfast of toast and coffee, and then I took the two small bags and the large shopping bag. Taking a taxi to the Cohen brothers' shop, I knocked loudly on the door, and seconds later a slit opened. I heard shouting from inside, and the door was opened by Danny Cohen, who hugged me and kissed both cheeks—*I just hoped that was a French thing.*

'Come in, come in,' he glanced at Olive. 'And your wife, such a lovely girl.' Olive frowned, and raised her voice,

'I am not his wife!'

We walked through the rooms to the large room at the back. Danny opened the door and there sat Moshe with a huge salt beef sandwich in his hand. Nodding a welcome and then putting his glasses on, he spoke to me in Yiddish, shaking my head and replying,

'I don't understand what you said.' Olive muttered,

'He said, 'George, you have come back like you said you would, hallelujah, please join us…'

I was puzzled.

'How do you know what he said?' Olive looked around, lowered her voice, and said,

'George, I am from an orthodox Hasidic Jewish family, my brother is a rabbi. I was only allowed to speak Yiddish in the family house.'…I was still stared at Olive in wonder. As Danny shouted for coffee, and we all sat. Danny sounded excited as he asked,

'Moshe would like to see what you have brought him.'

I emptied the small bag onto the table, and four stones tumbled out. Everyone around the table got their eyeglasses out to inspect the stones. Moshe was constantly speaking to Danny, Olive sat close to me and whispered,

'He said they are good quality, except for one.'

After much staring through magnifying glasses, Moshe left three of the stones on the table and put one back in the bag,

I took the other bag out and emptied it onto the table and everyone eagerly studied the stones.

Moshe spoke to Danny, and Olive whispered,

'He said, much better, but one is only industrial-grade.' Moshe put one back in the bag. Danny asked,

'Have you more?' I nodded,

'Yes, but let's see how much these are worth.' Moshe spoke to Danny again, Olive whispered,

'He told Danny to try one hundred and twenty thousand.'

Danny shook his head saying,

'Moshe is not impressed with the stones that you have brought, he was looking for better quality, but he will go to a maximum of one hundred thousand dollars,' and Olive whispered,

'Moshe said, offer one hundred and twenty thousand.'

Danny put his hands in the air and said,

'The best Moshe can do is one hundred thousand. Speaking loudly to Danny, I said,

'I'd think they are worth more, maybe it's time to talk to another dealer.' He grabbed my arm. 'Wait George, I am going to take a risk, one hundred and twenty thousand, 'Deal?'

I shook his hand and leaned over the table shook Moshe's hand, then sat back and whispered to Olive,

'You just saved me twenty thousand dollars.' She smiled, and muttered,

'Do I get a bonus?'

More coffee and sandwiches arrived. Then I took out the last stone from my pocket. Moshe, Danny, and the guys all had a good look, Moshe made a fuss over the stone, he kept passing it to Danny, and speaking to him. I asked Olive,

'What did he say?'

Olive put a finger to her cheek,

'Am I getting a bonus?'

I was frustrated with her teasing,

'Yes woman, of course, now what did he say?'

Olive whispered in my ear,

128

'Basically, this one is a winner.'
Danny put on a serious face and held his hands together,

'Let's see what we have here, Moshe said for the three the offer is,' he paused for effect, 'One hundred and seventy thousand.'
He threw his hands out.—'Take it or leave it.' I felt an elbow poking my side.

'I'll take it. Deal.'

The money box was brought through, and two hundred and ninety thousand dollars were counted and put into my shopping bag,

'This last one' Danny gave a sly grin, 'How low will you go for friends,'

Moshe smiled, the other guys at the table smiled, Danny smiled and patted me on the back,

'You know that this one is the one we want.' Danny spoke with Moshe, and then said,

'I have a phone call to make.

'He went over into the corner and spoke on the phone in Yiddish. I put my hand over my mouth and whispered,

'Olive, can you catch what he is saying.' She moved over to a chair nearer the phone. Danny came back to the table and sat down. Olive sat next to me and whispered,

'I didn't catch the whole conversation, but Danny was asking someone if they wanted a share.' Moshe smiled and staring at Olive spoke to Danny. Olive giggled and then whispered,

'Moshe asked Danny, why does that bitch keep whispering to that fucking gentile robber.' I looked over to Moshe and smiled, he nodded and smiled back.

After an hour of small talk, and endless cups of coffee the door opened, and two guys came in.

I recognized them from my last trip, we shook hands then they spoke to Moshe and Danny. Olive whispered,

'They are agreeing on a cut, and one of the new guys is saying, 'Why don't we just kill this bandit and sell the girl to the Arabs.' Moshe told them, 'This gentile thief will bring us more stones till he is caught, and they shoot him!' Olive grinned and whispered,

'I wonder how much the Arabs will pay for me?'

Moshe spoke to the new guys and Danny. Olive said they are saying 'The stone is worth half a million uncut...what shall we offer?' They all sat down; Danny spoke as if addressing a crowd.

'We have all clubbed in and we will make you a fantastic offer, two hundred thousand, deal?'

I stood up and raised my voice,

'You insult me.' Then reached over the table picked up the stone and handing Olive the bag of cash, said,

'I think we should sleep on that offer.' A chorus of groans went around the table.

'No no' Danny sounded nervous as he said,

'Wait, let's finish the business today, Moshe and my father fly to Israel tomorrow to set up a diamond trading company, with this stone they would be taken seriously and impress the other traders, please wait till I speak to my colleagues.'

They huddled around the table again, and after much chattering, Olive whispered.

'They will offer three hundred and fifty thousand dollars—their final offer, and Moshe cursed us saying,' 'I hope the plague descends on him and his family.'

Gathering around the table. Danny stood with his arms open as if going to make a speech.

'OK George, Moshe wishes you and your lovely wife well and makes a final offer. Olive uttered,

'I am not his wife!'

'Four hundred and fifty thousand dollars,' he stuck out his hand. 'Deal.' I shook his hand.

The two men in black left and closed the door. Moshe stood up and began to speak to Danny. Olive interrupted and spoke in Yiddish to Moshe, Moshe looked shocked and fell back into his chair, clutching his chest. I thought that he had a heart attack.

'What did you say, Olive.' She stared at Moshe.

'I said that it was he who was the robber and that you were a good honest man and that the plague will descend on him for his lies.' Danny looked surprised, opening his arms he said,

'Is this a trick? You understood everything that was said.'

Then went over to Moshe who was foaming at the mouth. Moshe pulled a shawl over his head and started mumbling to himself.

The door opened and the two men in black came up to the table with a large leather bag. I handed over the stone to Danny and picked up the bag. Danny said

'Aren't you going to count it?' I shook my head,

'Why? I trust you.'

We left the shop with six hundred and fourteen thousand dollars! Olive and I got a taxi and went to the bank, I spoke to the young manager who took us into a side room, called in two girls and they started to count the money and tape it up in five-thousand-dollar bundles. The manager sent out for coffee and sandwiches. Olive stood and watched the girls count the money. The manager asked,

'You wish to add this to your account, sir.' I nodded,

'Yes please.' Twenty minutes later the girls had put all the money into metal boxes and had gone to the strong room. I handed the manager two, hundred-dollar bills,

'This is for your help,' He held a palm up and shook his head,

'Sir, there is no need, this is my job.' He peered over my shoulder then like a magician the notes 'disappeared' into his pocket.

Now I had one million four hundred and forty thousand dollars in this account, but how to get the money over to England?

We waved goodbye to a smiling young bank manager.

Next morning over breakfast, chatting about our good fortune when Danny walked in.

'George, Olive, Moshe has sent me to apologize, but I must tell you that business is business!' He sat at the table and ordered coffee. Then said,

'Moshe has given me a present for Olive, and hopes he is forgiven.' He took out a little box from his pocket. Handing it to Olive, 'It's not a bomb is it' she asked. We all laughed. She opened the box and pulled out a diamond pendant. Danny stood up and put the pendant around her neck.

Olive spoke to Danny in Yiddish.

'What did you say, Olive?' She said,

'I told him that Moshe was forgiven and wished him well on his trip to Israel.' Danny smiled,

'You must come back to the Chateau for a meal, Celine insists.' I looked at Olive, and she nodded, and said,

'We would love to.' The thought of seeing that beautiful woman again made me smile.

Chapter 21

Danny had brought the black Cadillac; the car was enormous, and Olive was duly impressed. We all sat in the front seat, we didn't bump over the lumps on the road, we glided over them, like a boat over waves. Olive fiddled with the radio for a French music channel.

Danny chatted to an inquisitive Olive in Yiddish the whole long journey. That bored me stiff, probably because I didn't understand a word said. We finally pulled up at the big iron gates, Danny leaned out the car window and pressed a small remote, the gates swung open, and we parked at the front of the Chateau.

He opened the front door and we all walked into the huge dining room, a door at the side of the room opened, and in walked Celine...holding her swollen belly!

'George!' She kissed my cheek, and I got a whiff of that expensive perfume, she kissed Olive French style, a kiss on both cheeks, Danny came in and we all sat down at that
huge dining table,

Danny kissed Celine, and proudly announced,

'We have been blessed with a child, after all these years, a miracle!' Celine said,

'Yes, a miracle,' and smiled.

We had a long-drawn-out feast, with four courses, and lots of conversation in English, French and Yiddish all spoken fluently by the beautiful Olive.

Danny produced his 'famous' Cuban cigar box and placed it on the table. Olive asked,

'May I have one?'

Danny was delighted to have a fellow cigar lover. Carefully choosing a cigar and snipping the end, he passed it to Olive who put it to her lips. Danny held the silver lighter as Olive took several puffs until the end glowed. *It reminded me of the Japanese tea ceremony!*

Celine came back with a tray containing a bowl of ice cubes, crystal glasses and a bottle of gold label Johnnie Walker, she whispered, 'I haven't forgotten.' Olive said,

'Celine, may I have a glass to go with this magical cigar?' Danny beamed.

Danny and Olive were chatting in French, about Middle East affairs, and blowing clouds of smoke into the ceiling. Celine sat next to me and lowered her voice,

'George, you have brought a lot of happiness to the Cohen family, nearly three million dollars in uncut diamonds.' she took my hand and patted her swollen belly, 'And an heir to the Cohen family. She leaned over and kissed my cheek.

After an hour it was bedtime, and both of us were drunk, Celine said,

'The maid has prepared a room for you; I'll show you the way.' We were led upstairs to a huge familiar-looking room, Celine said,

'Goodnight,' patted my bum, smiled, and said, 'Good luck!' When she had gone Olive got into bed and cattily remarked,

'That woman was making eyes at you. I suppose you have bonked her too.'

I frowned and said,

'Don't be silly, she is a happily married woman.' The next morning, we showered together without speaking. Downstairs was a table with coffee, toast, and eggs. Saying our goodbyes, we climbed into Danny's huge Cadillac and drove back to our hotel. We changed, (still not talking) paid the bill and took a taxi to the bank. I took out ten thousand dollars that was wrapped in a plastic bag and handed them to Olive, who looked surprised, as kissed her, and said,

'Your bonus!' She smiled, putting the money in her bag, then said in a Marilyn Munroe voice...'Darling, we must do this more often.'

We packed up and took a taxi to the airport. The next flight to London was in the morning, so we booked into the airport hotel, put our things in our room, and went to the bar. Olive said,

'I must go back to the university soon, what are you going to do?' I replied,

'I have a job in the Congo that pays well,' she nodded and patted her handbag,

'Thanks for the bonus.'

Then Olive took my hand and said,

'You know this can't go any further, my family would have a fit if they knew I had slept with a gentile, a non-Jew, they are very religious.' She grinned and lowered her voice, 'But I won't tell them if you don't!' She wrote her telephone number and address of her university and the telephone number of her mother's house in London. Putting the note into my pocket I said,

'Olive, any idea how I can get that money over to the UK?' She thought for a moment,

'My father has many contacts; I will speak to him.'

We finished our drinks and went up to bed, Olive cuddled me and then grinned,

'You gave me a bonus... here is your bonus,' handing me a condom.

In the morning we had breakfast, and went to the check-in, Olive muttered,

'I should have brought my grannie pants! I've ten thousand dollars in my bag.'

Customs waved Olive through as usual, but stopped me,

'Anything to declare sir,' I opened the bag, I still had the three stones, and thousands of dollars, 'How much money are you taking into the country, sir.' He was a young guy, with a look of pent-up energy, the kind of look that wanted promotion. I glanced into the bag,

'Ten thousand?' he shook his head,

'Come with me, sir!' He led me into a small room with a metal table and chairs. Taking out one of the stones, he stared for a moment and asked,

'What is this for?' I nervously declared,

'I am a palaeontologist. These are samples for my students.' Hoping that excuse would work again, he grinned,

'That must pay well,' and put the stone back. 'Well sir, it looks to me that you have exceeded the money allowance.' He started to take the money out of the bag, I put my hand onto his hand holding a wad of dollars,

'Wait a minute! Let's lighten the bag,' I put the money back into the bag, took three hundred dollars and put them in front of him. There was a moment of silence, then he stared at me and lowering his voice, said,

'Sir, are you attempting to bribe a customs officer,' I nodded, He picked up the three hundred dollars and left the room.

I thought this is it, five years in jail for attempted bribery. Twenty minutes later the door opened and the customs man returned, took a piece of chalk and marked my bag,

'Everything seems to be in order sir, come, let me escort you out,' I was in shock as we walked past the queue to the end of the barrier.

He shook my hand, and passed me a note, saying,

'If you should need any assistance in the future with your luggage sir.' He winked and whispered, 'There is a number on the note that may help you. 'Good day, sir!' He turned and walked away.

Chapter 22

As we boarded the flight to London, I told Olive about the corrupt customs guy, and she looked surprised,

'Brazzaville customs yes, but Antwerp?'

When we arrived at Heathrow, I found out that there was a direct flight to Brazzaville in the morning. Leaving my stuff in the room I met Olive at the bar, she was perched on a stool with her luggage. I kissed her cheek and ordered a couple of whiskies, then gave her the three stones that Moshe said were of poor quality,

'Olive, you might get a few bucks for these.' Shoving them into her bag, she said,

'George, will you visit me at university?'

'Of course, when I can get some time off.' We finished our drinks in silence, then it was time to go. Walking to the taxi rank. We kissed. No more words were spoken as she climbed into a taxi and with a wave was gone! I returned to the bar. Early next morning it was toast and coffee, and looking out the restaurant window at the rain. I had forgotten about the rain in England. Then a taxi to the airport and boarded the French Airlines Boeing for Brazzaville at Maya-Maya airport.

Several boring hours later I stepped off the plane into an oven of heat, it took me a day of trains and buses to reach the town of Mbuji-Mayi. I made my way up the dusty road to the compound and my barracks. There were Congolese soldiers everywhere. I passed the Brits guarding the barracks.

Went inside, put my bag under the bed got changed into my uniform and put on my belt with the pistol. I took a jeep down to the beer hall, this felt like home as Raj gave me a beer, and slapping my shoulder, said,

'Where have you been man?'

Spotting Stan at a table, I went over and sat. He was drunk as he mumbled.

'They don't respect me!'

He took a swig of his beer, and I nodded,

'Who doesn't respect you?'

'The other men,' he said. Then took another gulp, 'I am resigning my post,'

'Where is Denis?' I asked. He pointed to the end of the bar. I shoved my way through the crowd to Denis who was sitting on a couch with a Congolese girl on his lap. He saluted me, and said,

'I am glad that you are back.'

Pushing the girl off his lap he stood up, and went to the bar, and he told me that a war-lord had attacked the mine,

'They had shot two Brits, one in the leg and the other in the arm. The next day they came back to the mine, but we were ready and put up a wall of bullets, when the shooting stopped, we counted seven dead rebels outside the perimeter wire. They took their wounded away with them. But boss, we have very little ammo, and the guys don't fancy going back to the mine without backup and more ammo.'

'Where are the wounded Brits,' I asked. Denis said,

'One has made his way to Brazzaville airport to get back to the UK, the other guy is in the clinic in the shantytown.' I had a beer with Denis to get all the news, then went over to the Belgian officer's compound; it was surrounded by Congolese troops. I stood in his office, and asked,

'Where the hell is the backup? And ammo for those fucking useless antique rifles you gave us,' without replying he stood up and showed me into a large room that had uniforms, ammo boxes and large metal cupboards. He opened one of the cupboards, there were twenty brand-new American carbine rifles with boxes of ammo. And two machine guns with ammo! I was furious.

'Why didn't you give these out to my men when the rebels first came to the mine?' He lowered his head and muttered,

'I was following orders.'

I went to the door, turned, and said,

'I'll come and pick these up in the morning, I also need a mortar and shells if I am to keep these rebels out of the mine,' the officer nodded, and started writing.

'I'll send the request to Brazzaville,' he said, 'But I can't promise.' I paused, 'Also, a platoon of Congolese soldiers stationed at the mine, till things quieten down.' I left thinking this was more dangerous than .I first thought

The next morning, I took three guys and a couple of jeeps to the Officer's compound and collected the new carbines and ammo, handing the old rifles over to a silent Belgian.

Lining up the Brits. on the square outside the barracks to give them the new carbines and ammo. Denis was excited with his shiny new machine gun. I delivered a long pep talk about keeping alert, sticking together, etc, etc. There were eleven Brits lined up, with three more in the barracks suffering from the heat and too much beer, plus two at the mine on guard duty and one more in the shanty town clinic with a bullet wound.

We drove to the mine, and the guards at the gate said,

'All was quiet,' we checked our walkie-talkies, the miners had already arrived by bus and were working inside the mine. With the noise of the compressors and the huge generators, it seemed like a normal day. At around midday, we went in shifts to the canteen for coffee and sandwiches made by a couple of local women, when I heard gunfire, going outside, I saw some of my guys crouching down behind the sheds. At the perimeter wire were three rebels firing into the mine. They had no tactics, standing in the open in full view making themselves easy targets. I shouted at the guys,

'Shoot the bastards.' A sudden eruption of shooting started, and the three rebels lay dead behind the wire. Cautiously going over to the wire, I saw the dead rebels were kids with painted faces, they had modern FN automatic Belgian rifles.

I sent out a couple of Congolese soldiers to pick up the bodies and weapons.

Where was the rest of the rebels? There can't have been only three.

Everyone was jittery, some miners came out of the mine to see what the commotion was about. The last thing that I wanted was for the miners to stop working. The rest of the day was uneventful. We increased the night shift guards to six and made sure that the walkie-talkies were working. When the miners came out and stood by the wire for the usual search and the warning speech. One young miner came over and asked about the shooting, grinning as he told me.

'That we would have to pay extra if they were in danger.'

I went over to Nkomo, waiting in line for the bus,

'Have you any stones for me? I whispered.

He spoke out of the corner of his mouth,

'It's very difficult, the two South African engineer guys are everywhere, checking on what's been extracted,' he grinned, 'But Nkomo knows the mine, I have some stones hidden inside the mine, they have opened a new seam of blue stones.'

What! I could not believe my ears, the blue stones that Moshe raved about. Nkomo whispered,

'I will try and get onto that work detail, but there will be an informer in that group, and nobody knows who to trust.' I said,

'Nkomo, if you can get me a stone tomorrow, I will be here at the search, if you have a stone for me, put a cigarette behind your ear.'

The miners trudged onto the bus, driving away into the jungle. Before the rest of the Brits got into the jeeps, we did some rifle practice to make sure everyone was familiar with the new carbines.

Back at the barracks, two recruits were waiting for me, we shook hands. One of the new guys was an American, who told me that he was wanted in London by a drug gang over a deal that went wrong. He told me, 'He was keen to join the mercenary group to get away from trouble and guns?'

I called Denis over and told him to get them uniforms and carbines and fill them in on the information that they needed to be aware of, I whispered to Denis,

'No need to mention casualties.'

Strolling over to Rose's house, I had not seen her since returning. I knocked and walked in. Queenie and Asre were lying naked on the straw bed, smoking marijuana. Rose was at the table, with her glasses perched on the end of her nose reading a week-old French newspaper,

'George,' She got up and hugged me, 'Have you brought me a present?'

'Of course, would I forget,' I lied! I took out a fifty-dollar note, Rose snatched it stuffed it into the dress with a thousand pockets and hugged me again.

Queenie jumped out of bed, strolled over completely naked, and stuck her hand out.

'Where is my wedding present?' As I gave her a twenty-dollar bill, she turned and shouted to Asre in French, they both got dressed and left. Rose made some coffee and we got talking about the rebels. Rose told me that these rebels were led by General Knotom. Mobutu had him kicked out of the army for corruption, so he formed his own rebel army, and they are camped in the next village, some of the rebels came into town yesterday, to drink beer and chase the girls,' she laughed, 'They are jungle men, many of them can't even speak French. All General Knotom wants is money for him, beer, and girls for his men.' This news shocked me. I asked, 'What did the Congolese soldiers do when the rebels came here?'

Rose shook her head,

'Nothing, if the rebels don't cause them any trouble, they don't care, half of them come from the same ethnic tribe.'

I couldn't believe my ears.

I said goodnight to Rose who hugged me again, and said,

'Thanks for the gift,' then she grinned, 'I might buy a new husband.'

Back in the barracks, most of the guys had collapsed into bed, some had gone to the showers. The heat was oppressive, and the whole place stank from the latrines.

I drove into the shanty town to the small clinic that was manned by a French doctor and two Congolese nurses, I spoke to the Brit whom I recognized, it was the same guy who told me that when he returned to the UK, he was going to find his wife and her boyfriend and kill her! We spoke for a little while, then told him, 'I will pick you up on Saturday,' he nodded.

Speaking to the young French doctor who spoke excellent English with no hint of an accent. He told me that he had studied at one of London's teaching hospitals.

Talking to a nurse as she showed me the way out, I asked her,

'How did this young doctor end up in the middle of the Congo jungle,' she lowered her voice.

'He was struck off for performing an abortion on a girl who died.'

Returning to the barracks. Denis met me.

'George you must see this,' the American recruit was standing behind Denis and stepped forward, wearing a red bandana on his head, sunglasses, a bulletproof jacket and two strips of red paint on his cheeks. A carbine rifle was strapped across his chest.— 'Rambo!' we laughed,

'That is your name from now on—Rambo.'

He paused for a moment and said,

'I guess that's as good as Josiah,

We went to the mine the next morning along with twenty Congolese soldiers. Later that morning the screaming monkeys had warned us that something or somebody was coming through the jungle toward the mine. The attack started with the rebels running out of the jungle firing wildly and shouting.

Stopped at the wire fence, holding their rifles waist-high, shooting at anything in the clearing.

We mowed the first wave of bodies down, but they kept coming out of the jungle, shouting, and firing. Suddenly, I felt a searing pain in my leg and collapsed onto the dust.

I dropped my rifle and looked down at my leg, it looked as if it had been cut open with a knife, I felt dizzy and passed out to the sound of gunfire.

When I came to, a rebel tribesman was standing over me, pointing a rifle at my head, with another rebel on his knees searching my pockets. The guy was shouting at me in French, then leaned down and punched me in the face. Blood spurted from my nose. The other guy searching me had taken the few dollars that I had but had left me with my revolver and belt. The one with the rifle,
leaned down and punched me again, cursing in French.

I spat out a mouthful of blood and phlegm then Pushed his rifle to the side and drew my pistol at the same time. Shooting him twice he fell on top of me. The other rebel jumped off his knees and ran. I shot at him and missed, shooting again, he dropped to the ground clutching the few dollars. Pushing the dead guy off my chest I sat up and looked across towards the mine.

A hundred yards away, three Brits and half a dozen Congolese soldiers were sitting on the ground with their hands on their heads, standing over them was a rebel with a rifle, hearing the shots he turned and looked in my direction. I fired twice, and he staggered backwards and collapsed. The Brits and Congolese stood up and ran over to me, picking me up. I was dragged backwards, with my heels trailing in the dust to the gate. Looking back, there were bodies all over the yard.

Rebels were pouring out of the mine entrance and firing in our direction. Some of the Congolese soldiers had picked up rifles from the dead rebels and were shooting back and running out of the compound at the same time. I was being carried out by a Congolese soldier on one side and Rambo on the other—still wearing his sunglasses!

We stumbled out of the gates and along the jungle road to the sound of gunfire, when two trucks with Congolese soldiers came up the road, towards the mine. I passed out again.

I awoke lying on a trolly at the shanty town clinic, bodies were lying everywhere on the concrete floor. The young French doctor came up to me, his white medical smock was covered in blood. He spoke matter-of-factly.

'I will have to get the bullet out.'

A nurse with her uniform covered in blood put a mask over my face. Her face slowly faded into a cloud.

I came to in pain, aware of shouting and bright lights and to see the nurse smiling.

'We got the bullet out and stitched you up.'

My leg was covered in bandages, and Rambo was standing next to me as the doctor came over.

'Sorry, we need the trolley.' Rambo helped me off and stood me up. The doctor shook his head,

'I can't give you any painkillers; we have run out.'

There were a couple of bodies lying on the floor covered up with sheets, other guys with bandages on their heads and other parts of their bodies were sitting on the concrete floor. Rambo said,

'There is a Brit over there who wants to speak to you,'

he pointed to the young Brit who had recently joined us. I shuffled over with the help of Rambo and a pair of crutches.

He was leaning against the wall with a bandage around his head, he had been shot, and the bullet had scarred his head. He lifted the edge of the bandage to show me the row of stitches across his head.

'Well, what's wrong?' I asked.

He started to weep,

'What if my hair doesn't grow back?' I looked at the dead bodies on the floor, covered with white sheets. Rambo glanced at me.

'Is he serious?'

Hobbling out to a jeep, Rambo drove me back to the barracks and helped get me into bed, the pain was intense, but I thought of the bodies on the clinic floor and bit my lip. Rambo said,

'There are some women at the gate wanting to speak to you, shall I let them in?' Queenie and two other women came in with food and hot coffee.

I was half-awake with the pain when I said,

'Queenie, help me out of bed, I need to take a piss.'

She shoved me onto my back, and shouted,

'No. No, lie back.'

She pulled my shorts down and turned me over on my side, then guided my wedding tackle into a bucket. I let out a,

'Whoa, what a relief,' she grinned, then gave it a shake. The other women laughed; she passed the bucket to one of the other women who carried it away still laughing. Queenie pulled my pants up, rolled me back and said,

'There. There, all done.' The women were giggling. Rambo was sitting on a chair and said. 'Better her than me, Boss.' Queenie said,

'My mum will come and see you this evening.' I lay back and went instantly to sleep to the sound of laughter. I awoke with Murphy and Margaret the nun standing by my bed. Murphy said,

'Bejazes, he is back with the living, thank the lord.' Murphy said, 'That he was told that I had been shot at the mine, and he and Margaret came over to give the heathen the last rites.' Murphy held his arm in the air and shook his head.

'Now the lord is saving heathens.'

Then they went.

With the help of Rambo, I got out of bed, opened my metal chest from under my bed and took out the bottle of whisky that the Indian gun trader had given me, I took a swig to try and ease the pain in my leg, I offered the bottle to Rambo. Shaking his head and stepping back, said,

'No thanks, man. My pappy was a drinker,
and it ruined the family, I have never touched the stuff, nor ever smoked. No siree.'

We got into a jeep and Rambo strapped me in, and drove to the mine, hitting every bump and pothole on the way. Congolese soldiers were guarding the place, and some of the miners were sitting by little fires.

I saw Nkomo standing by the mine entrance, he had blood on his chest, and he saw me looking at his blood-stained tee shirt, He glanced down at the blood, and said,

'It is not my blood boss.'

Several dead miners were lying inside the entrance and over a dozen dead rebels, I tried to organize the situation, and waved over four Congolese soldiers,

'Take all the bodies into the middle of the compound, get as much ID as you can, then burn all of them.' The soldiers stood looking at me, I realized that none of them understood English.

I called an officer who spoke English and told him what I had said to his men. Going over to Nkomo, he looked around

then lowered his voice,

'Follow me.'

We walked into the darkness of the mine, with bulbs hanging from a long cable attached to the roof, Half of them were out. Walking into the darkness with water dripping down from the ceiling onto the stone floor. The smell of dust and stale water was everywhere. *How could anyone work down here all day?* Nkomo picked up an oil lamp and lit it, telling me,

'Nearly there.' We came to a part of the tunnel that stuck out from the rest. Nkomo pointed to a ledge in the rock and held the lamp closer to the wall. There was a glow from a thin crevice of blue and white rock. Nkomo reached into a crack in the wall and pulled out three stones, one of them was a grey, white stone, the other two had a blue tint, and one of the blue stones was the size of a small marble. In the dim light of the oil lamp, I marvelled at the beauty of the uncut diamond.

Shoving them in my pocket, we made our way out to the stench of burning bodies. Congolese soldiers had piled the bodies up, thrown petrol over them and lit the funeral pyre. It looked like a horror movie, with the soldiers standing back from the blaze and Smoking and talking, like it was just another afternoon.

Chapter 23

Back at the compound, there was a meeting with Bingo the Belgian officer and a Congolese officer. I struggled out of the jeep and with the aid of my crutches joined them. Bingo said,

'General Knotom has sent us an offer, ten million francs and he will leave us in peace...for now.' Franke, the Belgian officer put a phone to his chest, and said,

'I have been in touch with Brazzaville for help, but Mobutu has told me that we have enough troops to defeat the rebels. He said that. 'They are only jungle tribesmen with bows and arrows. What is there to fear?' His defence minister is keeping the bulk of the trained men to quell a mutiny by the army in a gold mine near the Capital. They haven't been paid for months, and have killed their commander and his right-hand man, a relative of the Mobutu family. Then went on a drunken rampage, massacring a nearby village of the commander's tribe.'

'General Knotom is arriving this afternoon for our answer.' I told Rambo,

'I am going to see a friend. I'll be back in time to meet the General.' I slowly made my way over the square to Rose's house. My leg was hurting, I knocked and went in, Rose said, 'I sent Queenie over to you, to see if you needed anything.' She grinned.

'Rose, I do have not much time, remember we buried a box in the back of the house? I need it now.'

We went out to the back and Rose scraped away some dirt and wood then opened a lid, and there was my box. I took out a grenade with the timer fitted and then put everything back as normal. Going back to Rose's table, I borrowed a small shoe box, wrapped the grenade in newspapers, and closed the lid. Thanked Rose and returned to the square where soldiers and security police were milling about.

Twenty minutes later a crowd of rifle-carrying boy soldiers, running alongside a jeep carrying General Knotom came out of the jungle, and into the square. The jeep was followed by more young rebels, many were wearing brand-new army boots and American steel helmets, and others were barefooted with feathers tied around their heads, all carrying modern rifles.

The General stepped from the jeep, he was dressed in a French General's uniform with three rows of medals, I noticed one was for long service to the post office.

He spoke to the Belgian officer, then Bingo, ignoring the Congolese officers. The General turned to me and spoke perfect English.

'So, English-man it is you that I must thank for our defeat at the mine.'

He then spoke to the Belgian officer in French, Bingo translated to me,

'The General says, ten million francs by tomorrow midday or,' he drew his finger across his throat.

The Belgian offered the General a cigar from his box, and the General politely said,

'Thank you.'

They both lit up and continued talking like old pals.

I moved to the rear of the crowd opened my box, set the timer for half an hour, pressed the red button, closed the box, and approached the jeep.

A rebel barred my way and shook his head,

'It's cigars for the General,' I loudly said.

The General heard me, turned around and nodded to the native. I put the box into the jeep under the seat at the back. The General kept chatting to the officer, who sent one of his adjutants back to his compound to fetch a bottle of brandy. I started to perspire, ten minutes later he returned with a bottle of champagne brandy, by now I was sweating.

The general took the bottle, held it up and read the label out loud. My hand fluttered and my heartrate climbed. He climbed into the jeep and waved goodbye, paused, and said,

'I will leave three of my soldiers to look after my interests,' he spoke to his men and three young rebels stayed behind, then the

General drove off with his bodyguards running alongside his jeep. Moments later they disappeared along the jungle road, and everyone was chatting about what had just

happened. I stood staring into the jungle road when there was a muffled rumble, and a thin column of smoke rose over the trees a long way in the jungle. The Belgian officer shouted.

'What happened?' I quickly replied.

'He has driven over one of his mines.'

They all nodded their heads.

Bingo and the other security guys grabbed the three rebels, took their rifles, tied them up to the pole in the square and proceeded to punch and kick them, standard practice with the security police.

Four Congolese soldiers took a jeep and went to investigate the explosion.

I often heard of boy *and sometimes girl soldiers* who were paid by the military and considered expendable. They were mostly untrained, unmanageable rabble intent on looting and killing. On one mission we were sent by a Belgian officer to put down a rebellion in a village that was being protected by a militia of boy soldiers, who hadn't been paid for months. Some Congolese soldiers and two

French weapon instructors were with them.

I gathered ten well-armed Brits, and three volunteer Congolese soldiers, into an ex-American yellow school bus and set off the eighty miles along beaten earth jungle tracks.

It was late afternoon when we stopped near a small wooden bridge, three hundred yards from the village. Standing on the wooden bridge three kids with rifles stared at us, not sure what to do. One of the kids wore a French football shirt and a red cap. I ordered everyone off the bus and take up defensive positions on either side of the road. In the distance, an open-top jeep with six guys and several screaming girls was driving around in circles, sending clouds of dust and some hens into the air. A Congolese soldier walked towards the bridge waving a white cloth. He was in conversation with the three guys when voices were raised. The kid wearing the football shirt crept behind the soldier, holding a machete. One of the Brits was a sniper in the army and was lying on the ground looking through the sights of his rifle.

As the kid raised the machete, a bullet passed through his skull, sending his cap into the air. All hell broke loose. The guys on the jeep leapt off it, letting it career into a hut. The two guys on the bridge stared at the body with half a skull missing, then fled screaming to the village, leaving their rifles on the bridge.

In the distance an old man shuffled to the centre of the village square, shielded his eyes, and stared for a moment at the European soldiers, then shuffled away followed by five noisy dogs.

A girl walked out of the village with a plastic water container and slid down the embankment to the stream, staring at us while filling the container. A Congolese soldier stood and shouted something to the girl. As a bullet sent up earth near his feet, he threw himself to the ground and the girl dropped the container and ran towards the village.

Crossing the bridge in daylight to reach the village would have been an easy target for the guys in the village, so, we waited till dusk, waded the stream, and spread out as we entered the village. I came to the first hut and wrenched the door open. A couple and two children huddled in a corner in the gloom of an oil lamp, the guy feverishly pointed to the next hut. I backed out and closed the door.

Figures were appearing at the doors holding rifles, with the light of the oil lamps behind them they were easy targets. Some ran into the jungle, others stepped out and fired blindly into the darkness, and the muzzle flashes gave away their position. It was all over in minutes with dead and dying. The dying was dispatched with a shot to the head, not exactly the Geneva Convention rules of warfare. But this was jungle warfare.

We found the French weapon instructors tied up in a hut, their faces were covered in blood and bruises. The older one told me that one of the leaders told him they demanded one million dollars by the weekend or they would be beheaded and their heads would be stuck on a pole. He pointed to two heads stuck on poles at the end of the square, and said, When the trouble began the Congolese soldiers fled.' He pointed at the heads again, 'Those two tried to reason with the kids.'

He nodded. 'We were lucky, they thought they would get a big ransom for Europeans.'

This was the Congo, where corruption, torture and killing were commonplace. We left a very nervous couple of Congolese soldiers to look after the villagers until help arrived, then got onto the bus and headed back to our home village.

In the morning there was shouting in the square, there was one rebel left tied to the pole, and two security policemen were holding Rose. Rambo and I went over and spoke with the police, they said they saw Rose cutting the rebels free, two had escaped and ran into the bush, but they had caught the third one.

'Let Rose go she is my friend.' I said,

The security men dragged Rose to the police compound, shouting at me,

'Speak to Bingo.'

I had a difficult time getting to Bingo's office on my crutches. Despite the guard's presence, I pushed my way in and entered the room where Bingo was reading newspapers.

'Bingo, Rose is my friend. 'I said,

Looking at papers on the desk, he said without looking up,

'She'll be shot tomorrow!' I was stunned, my voice was stuttering,

'Bingo if you shoot this woman tomorrow, I will cause you big trouble.' He smiled as he picked up the newspapers.

I left and went over to the Belgian officer's compound and hobbled into his office.

'What do you want George?' he said. I was out of breath when I said,

'Bingo told me that he is going to shoot Rose tomorrow.' He glanced with screwed-up eyes.

'Who is Rose?'

Sitting in his chair he waved his hand, 'Leave it to me, I'll have a word with him.'

The next morning there was a mob in the square, the news had travelled fast. I lined up ten Brits. with rifles in the square. Rambo and I stood close to the pole. Bingo led four security police and Rose into the square,

tying her to the post then Bingo pulled out his pistol, and waved it to the crowd.

Above the chatter, I shouted out the

order...ready. The ten Brits held their rifles in front and pulled the safety catches back.

Bingo paused then put his gun back in his belt. He shouted at a security man who pulled Rose's dress off her shoulders and down to her waist. Bingo picked up his cattle whip and quickly whipped her three times, Rose passed out at the second stroke, and as he lifted the whip again, I shouted,

'Aim!' The Brits pointed their rifles at Bingo. Guys standing beside Bingo quickly stepped away. The crowd was hushed as I shouted to Bingo,

'The next stroke will be your last on this Earth.'

He held the whip above his head for a second then slowly lowered it and threw it on the ground, the mob cheered. Queenie and two women cut Rose free and carried her off.

Bingo shouted out to some other security men, and they dragged the young rebel that they had caught that morning, blood was running from his nose and a cut on his cheek. He was wearing a French football shirt and gym shoes. As he collapsed at the pole. Bingo walked up to him, pulled out his gun and shot him twice. I screamed,

'Bastard! We don't shoot prisoners.'

Reaching for my revolver, Rambo held my hand from pulling the gun and said,

'It is done,' there was muted cheering from the crowd. Bingo looked at me and shouted,

'I am the law.'

Going back to the barracks, I pulled my chest from under the bed, put the stones into my bag and took out a thousand dollars. Rambo drove me to the clinic where there were still guys with bandages and arms with lines of stitches lying on the floor and the trolleys. I asked the nurse,

'Where is the doctor?' she pointed to a side room. The doctor was lying on the floor asleep; I shoved the thousand dollars down his shirt and left.

Rambo took me to the beer hall.

As Raj served me a beer, I gave a dry smile,

'I'll have a whisky with that, I've had a terrible day at the office!'

I downed the whisky and could not get the vision of Rose being whipped and the young rebel being shot. Rambo stood next to me, holding a glass of orange juice, I smiled,

'Rambo, why do you wear the sunglasses and the bandanna?'

'Part of the outfit man, Part of the outfit!'

My leg was hurting, so I drank myself into oblivion that night. The next morning, I was out on the square dishing out instructions.

'Look, guys, be alert.' But I have a feeling there won't be any more trouble. '

They set off in jeeps as I looked at the post in the square, to a dry patch of blood on the ground and a crumpled shoe.

I hobbled over to Rose's house, knocked, and went in, Queenie was sitting at the table with Asre, and Rose was sleeping in the straw bed, Queenie said that Asre had told her that Bingo was going to shoot Rose and that last night the Belgian officer had told Bingo not to kill her, but Bingo said that he made the law in this state, not the Belgians.

Queenie held a finger to her chin and said,

'George, would you have ordered your
men to shoot Bingo if he shot my mother?' I smiled,

'Of course,—with great pleasure!'

I asked Rambo;

'How would you like a little trip to Antwerp?' He thought for a moment,

'Sure man. Antwerp? Is that in Ireland?'

I arranged for Denis to take over while I was away and told the Belgian officer that my leg needed treatment in London.

I packed my bags with Rambo's help, and we made our way to Brazzaville for a flight, which wasn't till the next evening. We booked into the best hotel in Brazzaville, into a two-bedroomed, two-bathroom suite. I showered and changed, then hobbled to the bar.

The place was heaving with people, French, Belgian and American. Pushing my way through to the bar I ordered drinks, a beer for me and an orange juice for Rambo.

I was chatting with a bar hostess when out of the corner of my eye I saw Rambo with a beautiful Congolese girl, deep in conversation. The young French hostess asked what happened to my leg, and I told her that my pet lion got confused with feeding times. She looked puzzled and then told me since Mobutu took over, everything was up for grabs...at a price. That was why the American and French businessmen were here to see what was for grabs.

My leg was hurting, so I said goodnight and hobbled upstairs to bed.

I was awakened a few hours later with Rambo creeping in with the girl that I saw him with at the bar, she was drunk and giggling. They tiptoed to the next bedroom and quietly closed the door.

In the morning Rambo woke me up, saying,

'Hey, boss have you seen Alice?'

'Who,' I asked.

'The girl I was with has gone and so has my money, my wallet and my favourite ring.' I sat up and asked,

'Was she worth it,'

his face lit up with a grin.

155

'Hell, yes man.'

After breakfast, I went to a pharmacy, and he gave me some painkillers. The old chemist looked at my leg in silence. Taking his glasses off he said,

'You should go to a clinic with that leg, it looks like it has got an infection.'

Back at the hotel, I phoned Danny in Antwerp and told him our arrival time, Danny said that there was a change of plans, Moshe was in Tel Aviv, Israel, with some investors. Danny was going to meet us at Antwerp Airport and fly us to Tel Aviv to meet Moshe, and not to worry, Danny had all the papers to get us through to Israel.

We boarded the plane for Antwerp. Rambo grinned and said,

'Do you know this fact,' Grinning as he waited for a reply.

'What fact Rambo,' I asked. He went on,

'That you can fit Belgium in a corner of Texas.' Then leaned back in his seat with a smile. At Antwerp customs, we were stopped and asked a few questions, and then Danny appeared, he spoke with the customs officer and showed him some papers,
the customs guy took the papers and went to another older customs officer who glanced at the papers and nodded,

'Have a pleasant journey, sir.'

'We have no time to waste,' Danny said, 'Our flight leaves for Cyprus in one hour, and it's at the other end of the airport.' He took my bags, and with a shoulder to help from Rambo made our way to the Cyprus flight. We boarded, and out of breath with my leg aching, I ordered a whisky to wash down a couple of painkillers.

Chapter 24

I was still asleep when we landed in Cyprus, Danny shook me and said,

'There are two flights to Israel today, the next one is in two hours!' I was exhausted and in pain. I held onto the baggage, *besides, what else were we here for?* Rambo said,

'You don't look too good Boss.' I gave a weak smile and lifted my voice,

'I'll be OK when I get to Israel and get the deal done.'

Taking a taxi to the airport, the sun was shining in a clear blue sky, I was in too much pain to appreciate the view. We boarded the plane and landed at Ben Gurion airport an hour later. The place looked lovely, everything was clean, people smiled, and they looked like a younger generation. At customs, soldiers with rifles helped customs men pat everyone down. The guy at customs said.

'Open your baggage, please.'

Danny stepped forward holding up his hand.

'One-moment officer,' and handed him

sheets of documents, the officer read the papers, then disappeared into an office. Two soldiers with rifles stood behind us, a few moments later two customs officers came out of the office and handed Danny the documents, shook his hand and waved us through.

We hired a taxi that took us to a hotel near the beach. Danny was on the phone in the hotel lobby for a half-hour, we were at the bar, and we had not booked in yet, I ordered a double whisky to wash down the last painkiller pill, Danny came over,

'A car will pick you up in two hours at the front of the hotel.' he said,

Nodding while feeling drowsy, I booked two adjacent rooms. Handing Rambo, a fistful of American dollars I said,

'Rambo here is a couple of hundred dollars, go down to the marketplace and buy a small gun, one that will fit into your sock, if you can't find one, go to a toy store and buy a toy one that looked real! I am going to bed, I will wedge a chair behind the door, and knock four times so that I know it is you, good luck.' I collapsed onto the bed and was asleep in moments.'

An hour later I was awakened by Rambo knocking, I opened the door;

'How did you get on?

'I could not find a real one,' he said, 'But I got this one,' he opened a bag and took out a black realistic-looking handgun, I said,

'Good, stuff it down your sock.'

We went down to the front of the hotel with the bags. The car was waiting with two large guys, although the temperature was in the eighties The guys were dressed in dark suits and ties, wearing dark glasses that made them look like bodyguards. Without a word spoken they drove along the coast highway for twenty minutes, pulling up at a large apartment building. As we went up in the lift, *I had a bad feeling about this deal, I could not put my finger on it.*

The apartment door opened and sitting at a long dining table were Danny and Moshe with six other Hasidic Jews, mostly older men, dressed in black clothing and wide-brimmed hats. Some wore black and white shawls.

It took several minutes to shake everyone's hands. Danny whispered to me,

'Who is this?'

I explained that Rambo was helping me get around. One guy pointed to Rambo,

'I'll vouch for him.'

Danny nodded then explained,

'This time there will be an auction for your stones, this is the fairest way, payment will be by bank transfer with you holding the receipts. I've taken the liberty to have opened an account for you.'

Handing me a bank book, he shouted,

'Ok let us begin,'

I took the three white and grey stones and put them on the table, they were passed around for inspection and much discussion, one guy shouted,

'Fifty thousand for the three!' There was a moment of silence,

'Fifty-five, fifty-six, seventy, there was a silence, then the 'auctioneer' said,

'No more bids,' then a large man, one of the men who picked us up from the hotel gave one of the guys a small book, he put his glasses on and wrote on the page then tore the page out and handed it back to the big guy who left the room, the old man who bought the three stones took them and put them into his pocket. I pulled out the little blue stone, the chattering stopped as it was passed around the table with each guy examining it. Moshe called out,

'Four hundred and fifty thousand,'
another voice shouted,

'Five hundred thousand!' There was another moment's silence, then one of the old men shouted in a voice that seemed to break,

'Seven hundred thousand, last offer.' I nodded.

'Deal,' we shook hands, then he wrote on a piece of paper and handed it to Danny. Looking at Danny, I said,

'Where is my money?' Danny said,

'Come with me.' I picked up my bags and with Rambo's help we took the lift to the ground floor, walked out to a waiting car, and set off to the bank, ten minutes later we got out at a huge building with a bank on the ground floor. Danny showed us in, and he spoke to a manager, I showed him the bank card that Danny had given me, and the manager took us into a side room with a computer on a desk. Smiled and said,

'You have an account of Seven hundred and seventy thousand dollars would you like to make a withdrawal?' I shook my head,

'Not yet I don't like to carry bank books and bank papers around with me, I travel a lot!' The manager gave a knowing grin,

'I understand sir, we can arrange that now if you wish. He looked over my shoulder,

'If the other gentlemen will kindly leave the room.'

The manager spoke on a desk phone. Moments later an assistant came in through a side door carrying a small box, the manager opened the box and said,

'Take my pen and write your signature twice at the top OK, now on the keyboard press a five-digit number,' the numbers disappeared,

'Don't forget the numbers, sir,'

'I won't!' *It was my army number.* Feeling faint I leaning against a wall and muttered,

'Danny, I need some air.' He took me outside,
into the fresh air and asked,

'What's wrong George?'

'I had an accident and hurt my leg,..'I lied!

'I'll take him to a clinic.' Rambo said.

We called a cab and Danny told the driver where to go, then said,

'You have a number to reach me?'

We drove off along the beachfront with beautiful beaches and a blue sea. My eyes shut and I passed out from the pain. I awoke with two doctors shining a light into my eyes. Someone patted my cheek.

'Can you hear me?' I stared at two faces inches from my face. A voice sounded distant. 'You're in the operating theatre, you have a bad infection and the stitches have burst.

Sir, can you hear me? We may have to amputate the leg!' I blacked out again with pain and shock. I came to with a nurse slapping my cheeks. She was dressed in a white uniform and the surrounding walls were white. *Was I in heaven? Strange, I always thought that I would finish up somewhere hotter!* 'Come on, don't pretend that you are asleep,'

she laughed. 'The doctor will see you in a few minutes.' Rambo was sitting at the side of the bed looking serious,

'Sorry boss they cut your leg off,'...

'What!' I struggled to sit up and pull the sheet back, my leg was still there, covered in bandages. Rambo fell about laughing, I made a feeble attempt to slap him and said,

'Rambo you Bastard, I could have had a heart attack!'

The doctor explained it was not as bad as he had first thought, and said,

'You could leave the clinic tomorrow morning, they have arranged a wheelchair and I will have a list of tablets for you, but you must take it easy for a week to let things heal,' the doctor wagged his finger, and smiled,

'No hanky panky.' The nurse giggled. Rambo said,

'I'll pick you up in the morning,' and left.

That evening I got chatting with one of the hospital porters, a short Arab guy who told me the history of the town, from a watering hole for sheep herders to a huge modern city today, I said, 'There is something I need.'

His eyes narrowed as he whispered,

'Ali can get you anything,'

I reached into my bag for some money.

The next morning after a breakfast of porridge, spoon-fed by a gorgeous plump nurse with enormous boobs that started at her neck, I was shaved and generally pampered. I would have been happy to stay there for another week, but Rambo turned up to take me back to the hotel.

'How about a walk along the seashore after you have picked up the money from the bank,' he said,

'What money?' I asked.

'You said that you were going to return for a withdrawal?' said Rambo, I suddenly remembered,

'Yes, I may as well do it now.'

I slowly climbed into the wheelchair and off we went to the bank, Rambo asked,

'How is the leg,' pulling a face I muttered,

'Sore.'—but still there!

In the bank I was led to a side room.

'How can I be of assistance today sir,'

'I'll take fifty thousand dollars please.'

A girl brought the little metal box in, opened the lid, and stepped back. The manager said,

'Now put in the five-digit number at the bottom, and write your signature with your finger.

A red light turned to green,' he left and five minutes later came back with the money wrapped in thousand-dollar bundles. Stuffing the bundles into a bag, Rambo wheeled me out into the a street bathed in sunshine.

'It's a lovely day,' he said, 'Let's take a walk and get some fresh air.' I weakly nodded. We got into a taxi and Rambo said, 'I've been looking at the maps for around here, there is some beautiful cliff paths not too far from here.' He told the Taxi driver where to go. It was a drive past the beaches that led to a rocky area. We pulled up and Rambo pulled my wheelchair out, paid the taxi and started to push me along a cliff edge track.

He stopped ten minutes later at a cliff edge and stood in front of the wheelchair. Putting his hands on his hips, and said,

'Sorry boss, but it's the end of the line for you, I'll take the bag.'

I held the bag against my chest and said,

'Rambo, what was it you were wanted for in London,' he laughed,

'May as well tell you, I robbed an old lady who put up a fight to hold onto some sentimental necklace, so I strangled her.'

His face changed to a scowl.

'Now give me the bag and say goodbye to life.' As he stepped towards the wheelchair. I held up my hand.

'Rambo, Last night when you left, I sent a porter out to pick up something for me, you may as well have this.' I opened the bag and pulled out a Luger pistol...

'Goodbye Rambo.'

He had a shocked look as I shot him in the head. He staggered backwards, falling over the cliff edge. I sat for a moment listening to the sound of the ocean and watched the gulls wheeling overhead, then my mind returned to reality. Wiping the gun, I threw it after him.

I wheeled myself along the rough pitted path until I reached a couple of kids playing football. I shouted,

'Hey guys, want to earn ten bucks.'

They came running over. One kid said,

'Is it ten bucks each mister?' I nodded, dipped into my bag, I took out a fifty-dollar note, handed it to the biggest kid, and said,

'Here, you can share.' Four pairs of hands grabbed the note. one kid said,

'You want us to kill somebody?' They laughed, I smiled, muttering under my breath,

'No, that's my job!' The kids pushed me along the cliff edge until we reached the beach and a taxi, and I set off back to the hotel. In the hall, I rang Danny.

'Hey Danny, was everyone happy with the deals.' He sounded upbeat.

'They were delighted with the stones. Moshe asked if you would bring him some stones next time for old time's sake,'

'Of course, I said.

Then dropping my voice,

'Danny, I have a small problem,

the guy who was with me has shot himself,' there was a moment's silence. Then Danny asked,

'Where is he.' I described the place, and then said, 'He is at the bottom of the cliff.'

There was a pause, then in a quiet voice,

'Leave this matter with me...and stay shtum.' I breathed a sigh of relief.

'Thanks, bye Danny.'

I spent the next week relaxing at the hotel, reading on the balcony, and enjoying the view. My leg was almost back to normal at the end of the week, and I was getting bored. I missed the action, but now I had over two million, two hundred and ten thousand dollars in banks in Antwerp and Israel, plus money in a British bank from my wages in the Congo. staring at the beach, I wondered,

Should I risk it one more time, or was I getting greedy, should I buy a nice apartment on the beachfront here, and have a nice life? Or go back to the

heat, flies and poverty of the Congo? risking my life where life was cheap. But in my heart, I had grown fond of the place and people...and the diamonds.

The trouble was, I was not ready for the rocking chair, and knowing that in six months of easy living, I'd be looking for action or adventure. I decided on one last trip. I packed up my things, put the fifty thousand dollars
in my bag and hoped for the best at the airport.

At the reception desk, as I paid my bill, the girl behind the desk mentioned that,

'She hadn't seen your friend for a few days, I tried my New York accent,

'He is swimming with the fishes.'
She looked blank then smiled and said,

'Have a nice trip, sir.'
As I went through customs, the officer investigated my bag. He gave me a curious look and was about to say something when I held my breath and said,

'A successful business trip.'

He nodded and waved me through.
I flew to Cyprus and decided there was no hurry to get back. Booking into a sea-front holiday hotel, not as plush as some hotels, but more friendly. There was a carry-oaky in the lounge. I went to the bar and over a few whiskies started to relax. I was a little drunk when I staggered up to the small stage and volunteered to sing Dean Martin's Little Ole Wine-drinking Me. As I started to sing, a chubby red-haired girl got on the stage beside
me, and said,

'Mind if I join in.'
I nodded. We both sang together out of tune, and forgetting some of the words, but who cares, it was fun. The sparse applause lasted two seconds.

Going to the bar where there was a crowd of older married ladies getting drunk and singing naughty songs. The girl who sang with me came up to me.

'Mind if I join you.'

I bought her a drink and found a table. We sat close to each other, I asked,

'So where is your husband?
I noticed the white line where the wedding band should have been.'

'He will be arriving tomorrow,
she smiled, he had to stay for work.'

Over the evening we both got drunk. I finally said,

'Time for my bed.' I got up and headed for the lift, she followed me into the lift put her arms around my neck and kissed me. Struggling to get the key into the lock she took the key from me and opened the door. As we staggered in, she closed the door and then began to take her clothes off. As I fell onto the bed, she pulled my pants down to my ankles, climbed on board, and got to work.

I screwed my eyes shut and bit my lip then letting out a moan, she grunted,

'You're enjoying it too?' I squealed out,

'No...you're kneeling on my fucking bad leg!!'

The next day I had breakfast, paid the bill, and took a taxi to the airport.

I flew to Antwerp and rang Danny, who told me that he was back in Belgium.

'I will send a car for you,' Danny said.

The car duly arrived and drove me the long drive to Danny's Chateau, with the big iron gates that opened for me as soon as I got out of the car.

Danny was smiling as he strode down the driveway and hugged me.

'Welcome George, come in.' I was led into the dining room. Celine came over and kissed my cheek. I got a whiff of that perfume! She patted my arm and said,

'Sit down, there is someone I want you to meet.' She called out,

'Marie.' A little girl with dark curly locks and huge brown eyes came in carrying a doll. Celine said,

'Come and meet a friend of your father!' The little girl stared and shook my hand. Celine put the girl on her knee and then lifted her sweater saying.

'Look here George, Marie has a little mole on her hip in the shape of a heart.' She put the little girl down to play with her doll. After coffee, Celine went to take care of Marie.

Danny lit up one of his famous cigars, blowing smoke into the ceiling, in a quiet voice said.

'While you were in Israel, an American guy shot himself! We found out he was wanted for murder by the British police.' They put it down to suicide and closed the case.' Danny winked and blew more smoke to the ceiling. Celine joined us and we talked and drank coffee and whisky while Danny smoked cigars and told me that Moshe and his son, Danny's father, were living in Israel permanently and that he, Danny, was running the Antwerp business. Shaking his head,

'But now it is all lawyers and contracts, he said, with Moshe, it was a handshake and cash on the table. You know George you have made my grandfather even richer; he sold the blue diamond at auction in New York for over one million dollars. By the way, George, if you want to get anything through customs,' he lowered his voice,

'I have a contact at Antwerp airport, just let me know in advance.' I grinned,

'Anything Danny?' He grinned.

'Well, not anything as big as an Elephant!' We all laughed. After another coffee, Celine showed me to my room. It was quite familiar, she stopped at the doorway, looked over her shoulder, put her arms around me and gave me a long lingering kiss, and whispered,

'Goodnight.'

The next morning, I showered and took my bag with fifty thousand dollars downstairs for coffee and croissants, then Danny said,

'I am driving you to the airport,' I said my goodbyes to Celine and little Marie and got into the huge Cadillac, off we went with a wave goodbye. Danny asked,

'Are you going back to the Congo?' I nodded. Danny went on,

'Mobutu had two mine managers shot for smuggling stones, there is no mercy if you are caught, it is the Wild West there. Come and live in Antwerp, I will teach you the diamond trade,' he laughed, 'You'll be the first Gentile to work in the diamond centre!'

I told him that 'I was carrying fifty thousand dollars and I was nervous about the customs.' 'He smiled, 'Leave this to me. Have you a spare hundred bucks?'

We parked up at the Airport, Danny took my bag and the hundred dollars! I went through airport customs when a call came over the tannoy, 'Mr Stephen come to section Four, please?' A young girl in an airport uniform handed me my bag.

'Have a pleasant flight, sir.'

Chapter 25

The flight to Brazzaville was a nightmare. I was put next to a huge black woman who snored loudly, and only stopped snoring for a moment to fart almost as loudly, then back to snoring! I made a silent prayer that her husband was deaf and had no sense of smell.

I booked into the Airport hotel, showered, and changed. Even though I had not slept, I was wide awake, my leg was nearly healed, and the doctors at the Tel-Aviv hospital had done a good, but expensive Job. I took a taxi to the Universite Libre Du Congo. This was the university that Olive studied at. It was late, but I thought that I might get information on her address.

Inside the entrance to the university, was an information desk, with signs in French and English.

I spoke to the girl at the desk about the whereabouts of Madam Olive Goldberg, she checked her screen. She stared close to the screen making her face have a blue shade.

'Do you mean Professor Goldberg?'
I was stunned, was there no end to this woman's talents? The girl looked again at the screen, then ran her finger down the screen.

'Professor Goldberg is still in the University; she should be in the library.' Giving me directions to the library. I walked into a huge, musty-smelling room containing aisles with a million books.

The place was silent and seemed empty.

I sauntered between the silent rows of aisles, then I saw standing at a table a beautiful sight…Olive! She was poring over some documents with her back to me. Tiptoeing to the table, I put my hands over her eyes. She froze, then said,

'George?' She turned around and gave me a long soft kiss, I caught a sniff of a woman and expensive soap. I grinned.

'How did you know it was me?' She touched her nose. 'The Joop aftershave.' I kissed that lovely mouth again and squeezing her behind she moved away, and said,

'Wait, wait,' opening her bag she pulled out a condom. Smiling and waged her finger, said,

'Remember, safety first' Putting her bag onto the table, she pulled her marks and sparks knickers down to her knees, then leaned over the table. I quickly got on with the job at hand.

Suddenly a group of girls passed along the top aisle, they pointed and giggled, and walked past laughing...I hadn't reached the stop sign just yet.

Olive frowned and said,

'Well—there goes my reputation!'

As we walked out of the university past the receptionist area, two girls smiled at us and spoke in French to Olive. Outside I asked,'

'What did those girls say?'

She grinned and said,

'They asked me if I had got what I was looking for. Tomorrow, everyone at the University, down to the porters will know what we got up to in the library.'

We both laughed. I took Olive back to my hotel and we sat down for a meal. 'So, Madam Professor no less, what's next, President of France?' She replied smiling,

'It's just that I love to study, I am a geek for information.'

Reaching across the table I held her hand,

'You are the loveliest geek I have ever met!' She let go of my hand and suddenly burst into laughter, and said,

'I keep remembering the grannie pants.'

We both laughed over drinks at the bar, Olive pulled a serious face and said,

'I am soon to be married, my mother has found me a husband, he works at his family's finance house, I have spoken to him on the phone, he is a goofy guy and a virgin, but I'll fix that when I meet him.' She gave a sly smile and winked.

Pulling a photo from her bag and gave it to me. I said he was a very good-looking guy.

She looked surprised,

'Do you think so? He speaks Yiddish so that's a plus.' Handing the photo back I said,

'Olive, I could have done with your talents, I was doing a deal in Tel Aviv with Moshe and Danny, — oh, and they asked all about you.' I lied. She nodded;

'I would have loved to have been there with you. Anything exciting happened?'

'Well, some guy shot himself, and the police put it down as a suicide, I figured he had been dealing with Moshe!' We both laughed,

'And I was bitten by a mad dog!' She smiled,

'Don't you mean a mad woman?' I pulled up the leg of my trousers to show her a long red scar. Olive bent over and ran her finger down the scar. She straightened up, frowned, and said,

'That's not a bite, that is a bullet wound.'

'How do you know?' I asked.

She looked at me with a frown,

'I did some volunteer nursing at a Kinshasa hospital. Who shot you?' Grinning I said,

'I think it could have been your mother.' We finished the meal with a Johnnie Walker green label twelve-year-old malt. Olive whispered,

'I trust I will be staying the night?'

Leaning over and kissing her forehead I said, 'I was hoping you would say that.' She stood and smiled,

'Excuse me for a moment.'

'Where are you going Olive,' she laughed as she picked up her bag,

'To the pharmacy for some safety-first items,' I gave her a thumbs up. We took the lift to my room. I undressed and got into bed; Olive was in the bathroom.

Someone was shaking me. It took a second for my eyes to focus.

'Time for breakfast.' Said Olive. 'You zonked out on me; you must have been very tired?' I hugged and kissed her, and said,

'I don't feel hungry for breakfast, do you?' She smiled and pushed me away saying,

'Wait... safety first!'

Managing to get downstairs for lunch, I asked Olive,

'What about university?' She paused for a moment

'There's no lectures till evening,' then said, 'It will give the gossips a chance to find another scandal.' She smiled. 'Besides, the university is very French in its attitude to these matters.'

Sitting in the hotel restaurant, I casually said to Olive,

'I am leaving for Mbuji-Mayi tomorrow.' Her face looked shocked as she said,

'What! what!' She stopped eating and looked at me. 'That is the most dangerous place in the whole of the Congo! There is a war going on there, the French papers are full of reports of massacres. So now I know where those stones came from! Please don't go back.

'Why should you care Olive;' I said, 'You are soon to be a respectable married woman?' She leaned over and kissed me,

'Forget the respectable bit, I have lots of friends in London and can borrow their flats for some 'unrespectable' sessions,' she laughed. We went upstairs to collect our things. While I was packing my things, Olive went in to use the toilet, she came out, put her arms around my neck and grinned...

'Oops, I forgot to put on my pants.' We both fell back into bed. An hour later we came up for air, we were covered in sweat. I reached into my bag took out a bundle with five thousand dollars, handed it to her and said, 'Here, my wedding present.'

She went quiet for a moment,

'Bless you George, but my soon-to-be husband is a millionaire, my mother chose well.' She kissed me and then said, 'You could have hired a top-class hooker for a tenth of this bundle,' I kissed her again and said,

'If she was as half as beautiful and smart as you, I would have given her two bundles.'

Olive stared for a second,

'George, have you considered converting to Judaism,' I pretended to choke,

'No Olive I am a born-again atheist. After a coffee. Putting Olive into a taxi, and with a farewell wave, I took another one to the rail station, on my long journey back to the diamond mines and 'home!'

Chapter 26

Sitting at the half-empty bar watching Congolese soldiers playing cards. A girl sat down beside me and tapped my arm.

'I am Shan, mind if I join you.' I turned to see a beautiful Indian girl with black hair down to her waist, and almond-brown eyes, wearing a flower print sari.

I needed female company while debating with myself whether to grab what I had 'salted' away and have a stress-free life far from the heat and endless flies, or to make one more trip with stones to sell and risk getting caught and being shot or a lifetime in a stinking African prison.

Talking to Shan, I learned that she was married to a Congolese major serving as a bodyguard to the president in Kinshasa and only came home every couple of months. She told me that she won't join him because her father was ill and won't leave the village. Shan sat close to me rubbed my leg and smiling said, 'Do you think I'm pretty?' I was a little puzzled, 'Yeah, I think you are beautiful.'

I was feeling uneasy when she whispered,

'Would you like a girlfriend for an hour or two.' So, that was it, she was a hooker!

I laughed, and said,

'Thanks, but I am waiting for someone.'

Without another word being said she went to the bar and spoke to Franke, the Belgium officer, then came back with a beer for me.

She smiled showing perfect white teeth, then said,

'I am going now, but if you should ever need me'...she put a card onto the table, then went back to the bar and Franke. Moments later they left.

One afternoon I drove into the compound and was surprised to see the place full of Congolese soldiers and many more in plain clothes, all of them heavily armed.

Bingo was organizing two young security guys that were hanging huge portraits of Mobutu on the wire fencing around the compound. The locals who lived next to the compounds were paid to hang bunting with the Congolese flag around the houses. As I chatted to him, he told me that Mobutu's son was coming to visit the mine in two days, using this place as a base to visit other smaller mines.

An open truck full of soldiers pulled into the square, a Belgian colonel in full dress uniform stepped out of the passenger side and barked orders in French. The soldiers lined up with rifles at the slope. I could see these were regular soldiers, probably picked for bodyguard service, and paid double the rate—regularly.
Twenty minutes later, a column of vehicles sped out of the jungle 'road' led by a camouflaged ex-British scout car. They came to a halt in a cloud of dust. One of the Range Rovers was immediately surrounded by soldiers. The officer opened the door, stepped back, and saluted as Mobutu's son, Kongutu Mobutu, stepped out. A short stocky man with a wispy beard and wearing a leopard-skin hat, carrying a sergeant major's stick with lions' hair sticking out from the end. We all shook hands and he spoke in perfect English to the officer.
Standing at the side of four grey-coloured Range Rovers were Franke and Bingo chatting to Mobutu's son who turned to the crowd waved his baton and shouted in English for our benefit,

'Keep the mine safe from thieves, the government needs the income from Diamonds to modernise our country, educate our children and provide a health system for all.' he spoke in a monotone voice as if he had said those words a thousand times before. There was flashes of cameras and interviews with prepared questions from the plain clothes guys.

Locals were paid to face the cameras and tell lies about government hospitals—that didn't exist.
As the light faded everything wrapped up and the cameramen and most of the soldiers headed for the beer hall...and the girls. Kongutu Mobutu, Franke, Bingo and I went to Franke's

compound with two bodyguards. Standing at the entrance door were Shan and another Indian girl holding trays of drinks. Hired by Franke to serve drinks to his guests.

We sat around an office desk chatting and being served drinks and food by Shan and her young friend Lucy, another Indian girl. Kongutu was drunk when he stood banged the table, and raising his glass, shouted,

'Toast to my honourable father, the president, and father of the Congo nation.'

He slurred when he told everybody to leave the room except Franke.

Walking out into the cool evening and creeping around to the back of the compound I peeked into the office window and watched Kongutu push a brown package across the desk to Franke, who gave Kongutu a small pouch which he opened onto the desk. The door opened and Shan and Lucy walked in with trays of drinks. Kongutu shouted.

'Get out, get out now.'

I was interrupted when a bodyguard strolled around the corner of the building, he pointed his rifle and motioned me to leave. The next day I looked at the card that Shan had given me. Parking outside a small concrete block 'bungalow.' I recognised the jeep parked at the side of the garden. Minutes later Franke stepped out holding his shirt and gun belt, jumping into his jeep. Waving to Shan who was leaning on the door frame. The jeep disappeared in a cloud of dust.

Shan beckoned me into the cool air-conditioned room. The bedroom door opened, and Lucy, her young friend strolled in carrying a tiny dog wrapped in a shawl like a baby. Shan made coffee and we sat around the tiny table. Lucy carried the dog to the door and said,

'Time for pee-pees.' When she left and the door closed, I leaned over and said,

'Shan, I need to know what was in that pouch that Franke gave to Kongutu?' She took a sip of coffee, grinned then said.

'I thought for a moment you wanted me...not information.' She took another sip, 'You will have to speak to Lucy, she was the last one to leave the room.'

Lucy came in with the dog and put it into the bedroom then sat with us. I asked,

'I need to know what was in the pouch.' There was a sound of desperation as I spoke.

Lucy smirked and put a finger to her chin.

'What's it worth.' They both laughed at my awkwardness. I pulled out a twenty-dollar note. She smiled and patted my shoulder,

'That's a good start.' I was getting frustrated with the teasing. I banged the table,

'Ok, how much?'

Lucy took the twenty dollars off the table then said with a grin,

'Just because you're our friend...it was a bag of diamonds with a blue shade.' I Slapped the table, 'I knew it! Someone at the mine was smuggling the blue diamonds to Franke, the Officer in charge of the whole operation.'

I held Shan's hand and lowered my voice,

'If you help me, I'll give you a couple of thousand dollars each.' Shan glanced at Lucy and said in a loud voice.

'No need to whisper, we share everything... even men!' They laughed and high-fived each other. I gave Shan another twenty dollars to buy a pouch from the market, like the one she saw in Franke's office.

Chapter 27

At the beer hall, I bought Raj a drink and then started to tell him about the recent visit of Mobutu's son. He took a long drink put the empty glass on the bar and smiling said. 'Look—what is it you want?' I put on my serious face,

'Where can I get a rear door key for a Range Rover.' He straightened up and laughed, then shouted to a little old Arab,

'Ali, come here.' The little guy shuffled through the crowd holding up a glass of beer above his head.

'Ali, this is my friend George.'

We shook hands, then Raj went to speak to another customer.

I explained to Ali that I needed a key to open the rear door of a Range Rover. He grinned, took a drink, and said, 'Where have you been for the last twenty years, there are no door keys, they are opened with a fob, and each one is different, what you want is a 'master key' that the garages use when the owner loses his fob.' He took another gulp of beer.

'I can get you one, but it will cost you,' he paused, 'There is nothing for nothing in this town' I nodded. *Now where have I heard that before.* Fifty dollars changed hands then he pushed through the crowd.

Chapter 28

Lying awake staring at the mosquitos buzzing around the tin ceiling, trying to get a plan in my head to steal the blue diamonds, it would be my exit from the Congo and into a life of luxury. I had seen too many deaths, and came close to losing my own life too many times, plus, I had lost the excitement for the job. I had everything working like clockwork so I could hand over the running of the security to one of the Brits. And a good excuse for leaving.

The Range Rovers and the Kongutu 'circus' were gone for two days to visit other mines for the usual speeches, and press interviews. Raj called me over and shouted above the crowd of drinkers, '

It's from Ali.' Handing me a paper bag. I found a corner table and opened the bag, out spilt a small fob and a set of three car keys.

During the day Kongutu and the cameramen, security and hangers-on had returned. That night everyone had gone to the beer hall, leaving a row of four Range Rovers parked in the shadows of the compound. One particular vehicle was guarded by two plainclothes Congolese soldiers carrying assault rifles, part of Kongutu's security team. Hiding in the darkness, across the square from the vehicles. Shan and Lucy crouched with me as I quietly explained the plan. Lucy giggled and Shan kissed my nose. I had a feeling they were trying to embarrass me. In the darkness only lit by a full moon flitting between the trees, I stood in the shadows and watched as the girls strolled over to the guards leaning against the Range Rover. After some talking and laughing, Lucy walked into the bush with the younger guard who propped his rifle against the vehicle. Shan took the older guy's arm and wanted him to follow her into the bush, but he shook his head and refused to leave the vehicle. She took his arm and led him to the front of the vehicle.

In the darkness I bent low and crept across the square to the back of the vehicle. Peeking through the back window, Shan had her arms around the neck of the Congolese guard and was kissing his cheek. Once more she held his arm and tried to pull him away into the bush, but he resisted. I crept to the rear of the Rang-Rover.

I pressed the button on the fob, there was a click so loud that I felt sure the guard heard it. I froze and then slowly peeked through the back window.

The guy was leaning back against the bonnet with his head back and I couldn't see the top of Shan's head...She was on her knees. The fob didn't work so I tried the master keys. In the gloom, it took me a minute to find the tiny lock. The first key jammed, and it took me a nervous two minutes to get it out without making a noise, the second one went in and smoothly turned.

A gentle 'click' and the half-back door silently swung up. Inside was the smell of worn clothes. Brown paper parcels of American dollars wrapped in plastic bands were scattered on the floor. After feeling around, I felt the pouch of diamonds. Stuffing it into my shorts, I replaced it with a pouch of low-value industrial diamonds. The door closed with a gentle click.

As I crept back to the other side of the square. I saw that Shan was standing up and helping the guy pull his shorts up. Lucy was standing beside them lighting a cigarette.

Back at the barracks, I emptied the pouch onto the bed, in the half-light of low-power bulbs, four large blue diamonds tumbled onto the bed. I stared at the blue tint glinting through the rough uncut stones and began to understand why people would kill for them. If I could get these to Danny Cohen in Antwerp, I could escape my life in the Congo and live somewhere in luxury. I'd had enough adventures to last a lifetime.

I handed over my command to Denis, visited Rose and gave her a thousand dollars.

She had acquired a new 'husband.' Queenie had thrown Asre out and installed an ex-boyfriend who looked like her husband's twin.

Driving to Shan's bungalow, she was in bed with Lucy both smoking long spiffs, and a young Congolese soldier was lying between them. I sat at the table as Lucy got out of bed completely naked and went into the kitchen and shouted,

'Coffee.' Shan crawled out of bed, wrapped a towel around her and joined me. Lucy returned with coffee still completely naked and joined us.

Over coffee, I told her that everything had gone smoothly thanks to their 'help.' I finished the coffee and passed her a bag containing five thousand dollars. As I stood to leave, Lucy nodded to the bed, and with a sly grin said.

'Want to join us?'

I awoke at dawn and threw my bag into the back of my jeep. With a special pocket sewn into my sock to hold the diamonds. Deciding to take my chances at the customs, I drove through the jungle on my way to the airport.

It was the following afternoon when I pulled into the gigantic parking area of Brazzaville airport.

For an impoverished African state, I marvelled at the Cadillacs, BMWs and gleaming Bentleys parked there. Walking to the airport hotel I booked a room. The young slim female receptionist looked at my dust-covered figure with a sour face.

'And how long will you be staying sir?'

Taking a shower, watching the water turn grey as it washed the dust from my body. I sprayed the aftershave all over my body till the room stank like a bordello, then crashed into bed.

The bright sunlight made me cover my eyes with my hand. I had slept through to the following afternoon. Getting dressed and putting on a crisp new shirt was a nice feeling.

Downstairs, in a crowded bar that was full of Belgian engineers and Congolese businessmen with a dozen or so well-dressed women. I ordered a whisky and checked with the barman who told me that the next flight to London was in the morning. A tap on my shoulder made me turn around, and look into the face of the young receptionist. She looked even thinner, with blonde hair hanging over her shoulders in pigtails. Grinning as she said.

'Buy me a drink?'

The girl smiled showing braces, and said,

'My boyfriend has let me down.' I shook her hand,

'I am Santa.' She nodded

'You can call me Pute'. She giggled and held her hand over her mouth, hiding her metal braces, 'That's what my boyfriend calls me.'

Ordering a cocktail, she leaned over the bar and told the young black barman exactly how she wanted it made, then told me that it was her night off and she was bored. she gulped the cocktail down, wiped her mouth with the back of her hand, paused and burped, grinning saying,

'Sorry, buy me another? I asked,

'Where's your boyfriend.' She grinned,

'Another drink and I'll tell you anything you want to know.' Sipping the drink, she told me he was a middle-aged Congolese guy working as a customs officer, she burped again,

'I only go with him because he gives me stuff that he has confiscated from the passengers, I sell the articles and split the money with him.' She grinned again and lowering her voice, said,

'He thinks that he is getting half! All the customs men do it and my boyfriend is the chief officer who takes a cut off everybody.'

Was I hearing right? If I could get this guy to wave me through, I wouldn't have to worry about getting searched, if they found me smuggling diamonds it could be a death sentence or at least twenty years in an African prison! I sat thinking, could I trust her? I had to take the risk.

'Pute, my lovely, have another.'

I pulled her arm over to a corner table. The waiter struggled through the crowd with more drinks. Clinking glasses I said,

181

'Tell me more.' She grinned as she told me about passengers who were found smuggling drugs and how the customs men would demand a hefty bribe and then sometimes still hand them over to the security police. Then they would sell the stuff to a local drug gang and make a report of the drugs being destroyed. She laughed as she told me about the scams. Pausing with her glass in mid-air, her eyes narrowed. 'Have you something to get through customs?'

I picked up my glass of whisky and paused,

'Suppose I had something to hide?' I said,

She slapped my arm,

'You naughty boy. I knew you were up to no good.' Finishing her drink she whispered,

'Come on you can tell Pute.' By this time, she was 'merry' and spilling drinks on her blouse. She was drunk when she muttered,

'Come on and I'll show you what I've got to sell.'

I helped her out of the bar and into the lift. Pute lived in the hotel. On the fourth floor, she struggled to get the key in the lock. Staggered across the room dropping her handbag onto the floor, kicking her shoes off then collapsed onto the couch. I stood at the side of the table as snoring filled the room.

When I was sure she was asleep I searched the bedroom, the drawers were filled with boxes and bottles, mobile phones, and two Smith and Weston pearl-handled revolvers that had been confiscated from an unfortunate traveller. Nothing of interest to me. But then I spied a plastic pass card that allowed the holder into the airport's lounges and duty-free shops. The card would give me the freedom of the airport and let me through customs without being stopped. The trouble was the photo was of a middle-aged black man with a goatee beard. I knew that in my bag were a few spare passport photos that I could substitute. I slumped into an armchair next to a snoring body and fell instantly into a deep sleep.

The next thing I knew was Pute shaking my shoulder and shouting,

'Wake up and get out, my boyfriend will be here any moment.' She sounded frantic, 'If he finds you here, he will throw you out and beat me up.'

I staggered half-asleep to the door. In the lobby, the lift doors opened and an older Congolese guy with a goatee beard and wearing a black customs officer's uniform stepped out with an arm full of boxes.

Chapter 29

At the airport, it was an hour before my flight to Antwerp. In the duty-free, I bought a men's gift set of cologne and for five bucks got the girl at the desk to gift wrap it.

Wandering through the crowds towards the customs desk. Pute appeared, tapped my shoulder, and whispered.

'I've spoken to my boyfriend, he's on duty at the customs desk...What is it you want to get through the customs?'

Handing her the gift box, I whispered,

'This is my future.' She took the box and said, 'What is it?'

As she gently shook the box. I whispered,

'diamonds.' Her eyes widened.

Taking my arm, we walked to the customs desk where her boyfriend was waiting. Pute handed him the box and then stepped behind him. He had a fake puzzled look, that changed to a smirk as he asked,

'And what have we here, sir.' Something had gone wrong. I glanced at Pute; she had a wide grin...I had been set up! I hadn't noticed the two security men standing behind me. They grabbed me, saying,

'Come along, sir, or you'll miss your flight.' As I was being marched off, I turned to see Pute and her boyfriend waving the box and laughing. Pute shouted above the noise of the crowd,

'Thanks for the gift...Au revoir.'

Sitting in a window seat as the plane taxied for take-off. An open-top jeep with Pute, her boyfriend and the two security men came racing up to the side of the plane alongside my window. Pute was waving the 'gift' box and mouthing curses...Pressing my face against the port hole I mouthed...'Au revoir.'

Letting out a deep breath as the seatbelt sign blinked off, I felt down my sock to the diamonds, and stretched into the leather seat, falling asleep with a smile.

I reached Antwerp and Danny Cohen, who bought one of the diamonds. Then we both flew to Israel to meet Moshe, who arranged a sale of the other diamonds. A week later I left Israel, two million dollars richer and with a nice tan. returning to the Congo................

George worked at the mine for another two years, accumulating another seven and a half million dollars in bank deposits. Eventually, he was betrayed and caught with uncut stones, tried, and sentenced to death by firing squad. Nkomo and his brood escaped to Angola to live with one of his wives' families, who welcomed him...and his money, into the tribe. With the help of friends and hefty bribes, George escaped and fled to Israel, settling in Tel Aviv, and buying a beachside apartment, where he loved to entertain his guests with stories of daring and danger. Danny and Celine divorced; Danny went on to marry Celine's best friend.
Celine married a retired American banker and lives in Florida with Marie.
Olive married her mother's choice of husband, becoming the mother of twins...safety first?
George married Doctor Elizabeth Pascal an American doctor and lived happily ever after..........But that's another story!

The End

Rufusdog@live.co.uk

From the Author

Your voice truly matters, so if you enjoyed this novel, it would mean the world if you took a short minute to leave a heartfelt review on Amazon. Your kind feedback is very appreciated and so very important. Thank you so much for your time.

More Novels by G. Emslie.

San Mateo ss

Hit Man ss

Priest Killer ss

....
Hesitate...You're Gone

Dead or your Money back

Innocent Assassin

Le Congo

All can be found on Amazon

Printed in Great Britain
by Amazon